PASSIVITY TO E

A Living Skills Curriculum f

by
Melissa Fenton
assisted by
Pippa Hughes

published by:
The Royal Association for Disability and Rehabilitation
25 Mortimer Street, London W1N 8AB
Telephone: 01–637 5400

Director: George Wilson CBE

Sponsored by BP

Published 1989
ISBN 0 900270 53 5

ACKNOWLEDGEMENTS

The Royal Association for Disability and Rehabilitation (RADAR) gratefully acknowledges the financial support of BP which has enabled us to undertake this project.

We would like to thank the members of the Working Group, appointed by RADAR's Education and Training Committee, under whose guidance this book was prepared. The members of this group were:

    Kit Hartley – Chairperson   Claire Mitchelmore
    Roger Ashford   Tessa Murray
    Elizabeth Fanshaw   Yvonne Quinsey
    Felicity McElderry   Patricia Ruffell
    Judith Male   Linda Tuckey
    Bert Massie   Philip Watson

We also wish to thank all the disabled young people and their parents who gave up their valuable time to be interviewed and the dedicated interviewers who arranged and conducted the interviews, namely:

    Jackie Batchelor   Sally Denham-Cookes
    Christine Battison   Barbara Finney
    Elaine Brown   Sue Steele
    Margaret Bye

In addition, we wish to thank all the many others who generously assisted us. In particular, we would like to thank Dr Melvyn Kettle for his help in designing the questionnaire, analysing the data and commenting on the draft chapters; Caryl Lloyd, Sally O'Shea, Ros Sills, Pat Whitworth for commenting on the draft chapters and Pete Watson for editing the manuscript. Thanks are also extended to Sylvia Freeland for coding many of the questionnaires and Pat Tubbs and Danièle Watson for producing the typed drafts of the report in time to meet ever-shortening deadlines.

We would also like to thank Christine Beels, Barrie Hopson and Mike Scally of Lifeskills Associates for their permission to use their model and reproduce parts of their work.

Last, but by no means least, we would like to thank all those who participated in the study who are too numerous to mention by name – the researchers, headteachers, teachers, occupational therapists, physiotherapists, non-teaching assistants, residential care staff, nurses, specialist careers officers and especially the staff in the following schools:

    Chailey Heritage Craft School – East Sussex
    Dame Hannah Rogers School – Devon
    Fairfields School – Northamptonshire
    Gleadless Valley School – Yorkshire
    Impington Village College – Cambridgeshire
    Lancasterian School and Hostel – Manchester

Melissa Fenton
Pippa Hughes

FOREWORD

We were delighted to be invited to write the foreword to this book. The authors have taken our holographic model for Lifeskills teaching and adapted it expertly into a framework for examining the educational issues involved in working with young people with disabilities.

Neither of us is familiar with the particular problems of this group of young people, yet we were immediately struck with the parallels in dealing with able bodied young people. In this context the distinction made between handicap and disability is one that we believe can be extended metaphorically, if not literally, to all people. In our experience many youngsters are "handicapped" by what society, their families and they themselves do to them. In our model we talk about people being "depowered". If people are depowered by others or, indeed, by themselves, then the result is that they are undoubtedly disadvantaged.

In our work we make an impassioned plea for formal education to work for self-empowerment because so many hurdles block the route to that goal. Again, we discovered from this book that there are parallels with young people with disabilities. Teachers and parents, often from the best of motives attempt to direct young people's lives for them, instead of helping them develop the skills necessary for them to live their own lives. The authors discuss the importance of facilitating independence and they do so within the framework of their own value systems clearly stated. How refreshing to see authors be honest with their readers and state, in effect, "this is what we believe and everything that we have to say and our interpretation of the research data will be influenced accordingly – we think you, the reader, should know this".

The research data clearly demonstrates the importance of poor self-esteem and lack of motivation as factors for disabled people just as has been identified in numerous research studies on aspiration and achievement in all young people. Self-esteem can only develop through the acquisition of *skills for living* which cannot be given, directed or borrowed, but which have to be learned through youngsters being allowed to experiment, make mistakes and by being supported and coached through the process. This is so clearly aided or inhibited by adult expectations. Higher expectations equal higher achievements equal higher self-esteem. Simple! But life is not always so simple and it must be especially difficult for parents and teachers when confronted with the additional problems of physical handicap.

We particularly commend the authors' recommendations for more in-school professional development. This will enable the many issues raised by this book to be explored and built upon by the group of people who are, perhaps, best placed to promote self-empowerment.

Thank you, Melissa and Pippa for seeing the generalisability of our Lifeskills model to your work at RADAR, and for using it as a framework for your research. This book should be read not only by teachers working with young people with disabilities but by any teacher working with 14–18 year olds.

BARRIE HOPSON and MIKE SCALLY

CONTENTS

List of Figures **9**
List of Tables **10**
Glossary of Terms **11**
Aims of the Book **12**
How to Use the Book **13**

PART ONE
Re-Thinking Self-Care and Independence Training **15**

Chapter One – Setting the Context **17**

The Need for the Study **17**
What is Independence? **18**
The Beliefs on Which this Book is Based **19**
The Barriers to Independence and the Role of the Education System **20**
Individuals **24**
The Holographic Model of Living Skills **24**

Chapter Two – Methodology of Research **25**

Introduction **25**
The Purpose of the Research **25**
The National Picture **27**
Evaluating the Type of School Programmes **28**
Evaluating the Effectiveness of School Programmes **30**
The Subjects of the Research **33**
Summary **34**

Chapter Three – A Holographic Model of Living Skills **35**

The Aspects of the Holographic Model of Living Skills **38**

Chapter Four – Empowerment **42**

Self-Empowerment and Professionals **46**
Self-Empowerment and the Advocacy Movement **49**

PART TWO
Skills 51

Chapter Five – Developing Self 53
Developing a Positive Self-Image 54
Decision Making 58
Managing Emotions and Conflict 61
Managing Grief and Loss 63
Developing Sexuality 66

Chapter Six – Learning 72
Providing a Broad Range of Experiences 73
Information-Seeking Skills 77
Information 79

Chapter Seven – Relating 83
Relationships with Peers 84
Relationships with Parents 86
Relationships with Professionals 86
Concepts underlying Skill Development 87
Assertiveness 88
Communication Skills 90
Giving and Receiving Feedback 91
Giving and Receiving, Asking for and Rejecting Help 92
Managing Conflict in Relationships 93
Ending Relationships 93
Relationships Skills Training 93

Chapter Eight – Working and Playing 95
Time Management 96
Maintenance Time Skills 97
Self-Care 100
Staff Issues Concerning Intimate Care Practice 108
Health Management 110
Mobility 115
Home Management 119
Leisure Time 123
Sold Time 125

PART THREE
Implementing the Model 131

Chapter Nine – Practical Curriculum Issues 133

Ordinary Schools 134
Special Schools 137
Introducing and Evaluating a Skills for Living Curriculum 138
Co-Ordination 139
Profiling: Assessment, Planning and Evaluating 141
Staff Support 145
Staff Training 146
Resources 148
National Issues 150
Summary 152

Chapter Ten – Parents 153

The Blame Game: Home–School Relations 154
Strategies for Home–School Liaison 156

Chapter Eleven – Recommendations 160

Recommendations for Action 160
Recommendations for Further Research 164

APPENDICES

Appendix 1 169
Useful Resources **169**
Lifeskills Teaching Programmes Nos 1, 2, 3 and 4 **169**
General Living Skills Programmes **170**
Disability Issues **174**
Developing Self **175**
Learning **177**
Relating **177**
Working and Playing **178**
Checklists **179**
Parents **179**
Staff Development and Programme Evaluation **180**

Appendix 2 181
Useful Addresses **181**
General Organisations **181**
Disability Organisations **183**
Genetic Counselling Centres **188**
American Disability Organisations **189**
Communication Aids Centres **189**

Appendix 3 190
Paradigm Shift **190**

Appendix 4 192
"Through the Looking Glass" – Reflections on Reality **192**

Appendix 5 198
Questionnaire for Parents to
Help in Planning Teaching Requirements Regarding Cooking Skills **198**

Appendix 6 201
Awards Schemes **201**

Appendix 7 214
"Skills for Adolescence" Curriculum and Pilot Scheme **214**

Appendix 8 216
Certificate of Pre-Vocational Education **216**

References 218

LIST OF FIGURES

Chapter Two

Fig 2.1 A Diagram Showing the Methodology of the Study **26**

Chapter Three

Fig 3.1 The Holographic Model of Living Skills (Depicted as a dodecahedron) **38**
Fig 3.2 The Skills Aspect of the Holographic Model **40**
Fig 3.3 Life Roles **41**

Chapter Four

Fig 4.1 Differentiation Between a More or Less Self-Empowered Person **43**
Fig 4.2 Fundamentals of Self-Empowered Behaviour **45**

Chapter Five

Fig 5.1 Mr and Mrs Wheely **55**
Fig 5.2 Painting **56**
Fig 5.3 The Logical Decision-Making Process **59**

Chapter Seven

Fig 7.1 Factors Involved in Social Isolation **85**
Fig 7.2 The Differences Between Assertion, Aggression and Non-assertion **88**

Chapter Eight

Fig 8.1 Maintenance Time Skills **98**

Chapter Nine

Fig 9.1 Confusion or Support? **140**
Fig 9.2 Suggestions for Staff Development Workshops **147**

Chapter Ten

Fig 10.1 The Blame Game **154**
Fig 10.2 Summary of Next Steps: A Workshop for Parents **159**

LIST OF TABLES

Chapter Two

Table 2.1 Types of Establishments Visited **29**
Table 2.2 Sections of Interview Schedule **30**
Table 2.3 Type of School and Geographic Area Involved in Structured Interviews **31**
Table 2.4 Numbers of Students in each Age Range **31**
Table 2.5 Main Impairments of Students **32**

Chapter Three

Table 3.1 Factors which Inhibit Independence **36**

Chapter Seven

Table 7.1 The Frequency of Contact with Peers Outside School Hours **84**
Table 7.2 The Desired Contact with Peers Outside School Hours **85**

Chapter Eight

Table 8.1 The Number of Schools with Paramedical Support **99**
Table 8.2 Bathing and Showering Practice at Initial Interview **102**
Table 8.3 Washing Hair Practice **103**
Table 8.4 Dressing Skills **104**
Table 8.5 Management of Bladder and Bowels **106**
Table 8.6 Negotiating Indoor Obstacles **115**
Table 8.7 Making Transfers from Wheelchairs **116**
Table 8.8 Negotiating Outdoor Obstacles **117**
Table 8.9 Making Hot Drinks, Snacks and Simple Meals **121**
Table 8.10 Involvement in Clubs **124**
Table 8.11 Post School Preferences **128**
Table 8.12 Post School Expectations **129**

Chapter Nine

Table 9.1 In-Service Training **146**
Table 9.2 School Staff that Receive Training **147**

GLOSSARY OF TERMS

Impairment: "A permanent or transitory psychological, physiological, or anatomical loss or abnormality of structure or function." *WHO (1980)*

Disability: "Any restriction or prevention of the performance of an activity, resulting from an impairment, in the manner or within the range considered normal for a human being." *WHO (1980)*

Handicap is defined as a dynamic relationship between the individual and his environment. The degree to which a disability is handicapping depends on the situations experienced by the individual, the attitudes and expectations of others and the intervention strategies and environmental modifications which are made. *OECD (1986)*

Independence: ". . . choosing how to live one's life within one's inherent capacities and means and consistent with one's personal values and preferences." *Turnbull and Turnbull (1985)*

Self-Empowerment: a process of becoming increasingly more in control of oneself and one's life, and thus increasingly more independent.

Parent: A mother/father, a guardian or carer who is fulfilling a parental role.

Professional: A member of staff within the educational system who is employed to provide a professional service to young people with disabilities. A partial list includes teacher, occupational therapist, speech therapist, physiotherapist, nurse, non-teaching assistant, care worker and social worker.

She and **Herself** should be read to mean the pronouns she and he, hers and his, and herself and himself respectively. Where this is not so, the distinction is obvious. This is done to avoid the convention of writing in the male gender and the laborious use of s/he, hers/his and herself/himself.

Student has been used throughout this book as it is increasingly common for young people in schools, aged 15/16, to be referred to as students. Thus, rather than alternating between "pupil" and "student", the term student has been used consistently.

AIMS OF THE BOOK

The question of independence has been central to the education of young people with disabilities for many years. Undoubtedly, strides are being made in this field through the use of task analysis and structured assessment and evaluation procedures, but despite this, there is much more to be done if young people with disabilities are to achieve their maximum levels of personal independence.

The book aims to build on existing good practice and to suggest the need to develop a wider notion of independence. Thus, the book emphasises the importance of developing psychological and social as well as physical independence. In doing this, we have six main objectives:

1. To examine, evaluate and document the "self-care and independence training" currently available.
2. To provide real evidence and information on the extent and effectiveness of the "self-care" and "independence" training currently available by using a variety of research techniques.
3. To build on current models of "self-care and independence training" and to highlight the need for choice and autonomy.
4. To emphasise that enabling young people with disabilities to become more independent involves a multifaceted process of development for all those involved.
5. To improve the explicit and hidden curricula within education establishments. (This includes course content and delivery of this content; assessment; planning and monitoring procedures; co-ordination of programmes; parental involvement; staff development and useful resources.)
6. To be a starting point for discussion of the complex issues involved: there are no blueprints for enabling young people with disabilities to become more independent.

HOW TO USE THE BOOK

This book is divided into three parts:

PART ONE – Re-Thinking Self-Care and Independence Training

The first part is an overall introduction:

Chapter One sets the context within which everyone is working and outlines the main disability issues. **Chapter Two** explains the methodology of the research study. **Chapter Three** introduces the advocated holographic model for facilitating independence in young people with disabilities. **Chapter Four** explores the concept of empowerment in terms of students with disabilities and in less detail, their parents, professionals working with them and the school system.

PART TWO – Skills

The second part discusses the SKILLS aspect of the model: **Chapter Five** looks at the skills involved in developing the self; **Chapter Six**, the skills of learning; **Chapter Seven**, the skills of relating and **Chapter Eight**, the skills of working and playing. There is no particular order to the learning of the skills, except where some will help in the acquisition of others. The individual's readiness to learn and her abilities and needs should determine the approach adopted. The results from the structured interview component of the research conducted with young people with disabilities and their parents are interspersed throughout **Chapters Six**, **Seven** and **Eight**.

PART THREE – Implementing the Model

The third and final part looks at the practical issues involved in implementing this holographic model of living skills in educational settings. **Chapter Nine** discusses Practical Curriculum Issues, **Chapter Ten** discusses working with parents, and **Chapter Eleven** is a list of recommendations for future action and research.

This book should be read as a whole. It is our contention that "independence training" must take place within a clear theoretical framework. In addition, the skills outlined in Part Two are directly related to the text in Part One. Although it is possible to pick and choose the skills applicable to each young person at any given time, it is important that the skills section is addressed within the context of the whole model:

"Skills taught without reference to values or to information can be dangerous to the person and the community. Values taught without skill development can result in total frustration" (Hopson and Scally 1987a).

PART ONE

Re-Thinking Self-Care and Independence Training

CHAPTER ONE
Setting the Context

THE NEED FOR THE STUDY

RADAR's concern with the independence of young people with disabilities was heightened by the results of two research studies: "Disability in Adolescence" (Anderson and Clarke 1982a) and "Beyond the School Gate" (Bookis 1983b).

The findings of these studies revealed that many disabled young people were likely to have difficulties in carrying out the basic activities of daily living: dressing, personal care and household tasks. It was recommended that they should receive more intensive "self-care and independence training" at school, as deficits in these skills would constitute a major handicap for them in their post-school lives.

Social isolation among the young people interviewed in both studies was another cause for concern. It seemed to arise primarily from four factors:
 - poor self-image,
 - lack of social skills,
 - inaccessible transport, and
 - inadequate knowledge and skills in arranging and/or using the available transport.

Furthermore, these studies showed not only a considerable lack of information among interviewees about the causes and effects of their specific impairments, but also little knowledge about the services and allowances to which they were entitled.

Any school curriculum working towards the independence of students with disabilities needs to address the issues raised above. It is from this point that this research study started three years ago, and since then, some special and ordinary schools have also begun to explore some of the critical issues.

WHAT IS INDEPENDENCE?

Independence, though highly valued in modern society is a nebulous concept. It is difficult to define and even more difficult to develop in educational settings. In the special education system, "independence" has come to mean the completion of physical tasks without assistance (Smith and Neisworth 1975). Thus, most independence training addresses the specific mechanical and operational skills which young people need, for example, self-care skills and activities of daily living. These skills are intended to help young people function in society to the "best" of their ability. To many, this means conducting tasks without assistance, being able to live alone, working in competitive employment, and developing and maintaining relationships with able-bodied peers.

Underlying much of this approach is the philosophy that people with disabilities have a pathology, the effects of which need to be minimised or "fixed" so that they can work towards the societal able-bodied norm. This approach has been labelled the "fix-it" model of independence (Turnbull and Turnbull 1985).

Adults with disabilities within the independent living movement have recently begun questioning this "fix-it" perspective on independence. They argue that by living according to this definition, they will always be "second best" to their able-bodied peers. In other words, whilst becoming more physically independent, they are also perpetuating their own social and psychological dependence. Therefore, they have adopted a perspective on independence which is sufficiently flexible to allow all individuals to explore what independence means for them – the "consent/choice/autonomy" perspective. Within this perspective, independence ultimately refers to self-direction (Zola 1983). The key to independence is choice: choosing to complete physical tasks without assistance or choosing to complete physical tasks with assistance whilst being in control of how and when that assistance is offered.

Turnbull and Turnbull (1985) developed the following definition of independence:

"... choosing how to live one's life within one's inherent capacities and means and consistent with one's personal values and preferences".

It is upon this definition and the beliefs outlined in the next section, that this book is based.

THE BELIEFS ON WHICH THIS BOOK IS BASED

Many people's beliefs are based on attitudes and policies established some years ago. These are increasingly being reviewed with the rise in expectations of people with disabilities and the wider range of opportunities available to meet these expectations. The beliefs on which this book is based are now expressed by some disability organisations. They form the foundation of the holographic model of living skills outlined in Chapter Three, and are identified in the following list. The list is not exhaustive, but covers the key issues pertinent to enabling students to become more independent. Some are general statements and others relate more specifically to people with disabilities.

The General Beliefs on Which this Book is Based

A   Each individual is unique, valuable and worthy of respect.

B   Education, therapy and self-empowerment are value-based.

C   The more self-empowered a person becomes, the more able she will be to enable others to be the same.

D   Once people have learned to respect, love and value themselves, they will be able to respect, love and value others.

E   It is helpful to differentiate between the behaviours which encourage the developing parts of a person, and those which serve to anchor her in states of depression, hostility, fear and/or insecurity.

F   The stages of bereavement are a useful tool for exploring many different kinds of loss. It is helpful to acknowledge loss and grief, and to learn to explore one's bereavement process.

G   Taking risks and learning from mistakes is effective and valuable.

H   Everyone has something to teach and something to learn.

I   Parents have a vital contribution to make along with those working towards the independence of their children.

The "Disability-Related" Beliefs on Which this Book is Based

A   Every young person should be seen as an individual who may or may not appear to fit the stereotype of her disability. Young people's self-image is generally affected by how they are described by others. The use of language is important.

B   There is a distinct difference between disability and handicap.

C   People with disabilities are depowered by society, and many are treated as second-class citizens.

D   The internalised oppression of people with disabilities can be actively explored and surmounted via group work and individual counselling.

E   People with disabilities are sexual beings who can choose their sexual orientation from a number of equally valid options.

F   Explaining traits, characteristics or behaviours, which may exist or may only be perceived to exist in a disabled person, solely in terms of an individual's impairment or disability is common, yet very often destructive. For example, if someone with a disability is angry or sad, then this is often related to her impairment. These same characteristics, however, would rarely be related to an able-bodied person's able-bodiedness.

G   It is divisive to propose curriculum change purely for young people with disabilities within the special education system. A living skills model for young people with disabilities should be equally appropriate to able-bodied young people in principle although each individual living skills programme may differ.

Having stated the beliefs on which this book is based, we will now examine some of the obstacles which young people face when striving for independence.

THE BARRIERS TO INDEPENDENCE AND THE ROLE OF THE EDUCATION SYSTEM

One of the prerequisites to independence within the framework outlined is that all young people have access to the same opportunities. This is not the case for the majority of young people with disabilities within Britain today. The following section identifies some of the major obstacles they face in their fight for independence.

Attitudinal Barriers

Negative attitudes towards disability are deeply inbred within our culture. In the past, cultural and religious doctrines have associated disability with evil, and physical impairments have been seen as a punishment for sin or misdeeds in a past life (Leahy 1982). Although modern doctrines may no longer subscribe to these associations, it can be argued that remnants of them still exist in a more subtle form.

Attitudes towards disability are probably the most insidious of the barriers that face people with disabilities. Ignorant distortions of the effect of any particular disability often generate devaluing reactions in able-bodied people, such as pity, avoidance, fear, intrusive curiosity and benevolence (Foster et al. 1977).

The general public tends to generalise the effects of one aspect of the individual to the whole person. The shopkeeper who reacts to the customer using a wheelchair as though she cannot hear, is one example. Young people and adults with physical disabilities are also frequently treated as though they are children. This may stem from the assumption that someone with a physical disability also has a mental impairment. However, is it appropriate to treat an adult with learning difficulties as a child? In general, society does not encourage young people with learning difficulties and/or physical disabilities to become more independent. This is probably because of fear and a lack of understanding of the issues.

Integrating children with disabilities, and developing courses between special and ordinary schools are positive contributions to changing society's attitudes. More able-bodied and disabled children are now interacting at an earlier age, so having the opportunity to dispel many of the myths surrounding disability. However, attitudes are slow to change and explicit disability awareness work can speed up this process (Quicke 1987).

Devaluing attitudes towards people with disabilities are an acute form of oppression. People with disabilities may have absorbed these oppressive attitudes and therefore could find it helpful to address them within themselves (see page 58). For example, western society places considerable value on stereotypical physical beauty: this stereotype has a considerable influence on the way people see themselves (Chapkif 1986). Many people's self-esteem, though not everyone's, would be threatened by any disability which affected the perceived ideal of physical beauty (Wright 1960).

Whilst these attitudes may be most prevalent amongst those who have no direct experience of disability, some devaluing attitudes are directly applicable to those working with people with disabilities. The term "iatrogenesis" was used by Illich (1975) to describe the dangers of the professionalisation of care. Although he stated that these counter-productive processes originated in the medical and paramedical professions, others have argued that they have spread into teaching (Hopson and Scally 1981a) and social work (Edwards 1985). Illich sub-divides iatrogenesis into three types: clinical, social and structural.

"Clinical iatrogenesis" is defined as the pain, sickness and death which can paradoxically be caused by or as a by-product of medical intervention, some of which he argues to be needless. "Social iatrogenesis" refers to a system which creates an artificial need for its services. In other words, help is offered to solve a problem which did not initially exist. Both these types of iatrogenesis can be usefully considered when working with young people with disabilities: what are the arguments for and against a young person having a proposed operation? Is the intervention really helpful in this instance? In "structural iatrogenesis", Illich argues that people are reduced to the status of passive consumers by undermining their competence in growing up and helping each other. People who have lost their sense of personal autonomy at an early age may be conditioned into perceiving professionals as knowing best. It is then very easy for professionals to support this belief thus perpetuating the cycle of the myth. There is a danger that teachers, paramedics and other service providers can become members of what Illich et al. (1977) term the "disabling professions", by inadvertently gaining professional esteem and personal security at the expense of the people with and for whom they are working.

The devaluing attitudes expressed by both the general public and professionals may leave some young people with disabilities believing themselves to have no control over their lives. These feelings of powerlessness can result in depression, a state which is likely to prevent them from reversing the process. In essence, if the devaluing attitudes are absorbed, they may be expressed through the process of "learned helplessness" (Seligman 1975). It is hoped that the model of living skills outlined in this book can enable young people to overcome some of the feelings of powerlessness they might have.

Environmental Barriers

It has been argued that disability itself is a socially defined problem (Finkelstein 1981). It is RADAR's policy to make a distinction between disability and handicap in the following way:
> "Whether a disabled person is also handicapped will depend upon the interaction between his/her functional loss and his/her surroundings . . ." Kettle (1979).

The terms disability and handicap cannot meaningfully be used interchangeably. To take public transport as an example: if bus stops and buses were accessible to all, those people who use wheelchairs would be disabled but not handicapped when travelling from A to B. Many people are handicapped by environmental barriers in society in that their needs are not taken into account in many public activities eg. in the design of public transport and buildings. People with disabilities are one minority group who do not have the same access to facilities as their able-bodied peers and thus are treated as though they are second-class citizens.

These environmental barriers cannot be affected directly by the educational process. However, an education process which empowers disabled young people would give them the choice of whether to accept passively the handicapping aspects of society, or to influence society and their role in it, and to seek to remove such handicaps.

Discrimination in Terms of Employment

Given the high rate of general unemployment and the attitudinal and environmental barriers outlined, many young people with disabilities will experience considerable discrimination within the employment market. For example, research has shown that many employers do not interview people with disabilities even if they are adequately qualified for the post (Fry 1986). Other research has revealed that those young people who enter sheltered employment are highly unlikely to be given the opportunity by employers to move into open employment: they have an approximately 3% chance of being able to move into open employment (Jones, Minns and Wright 1988). Although schools can do little to counter the prejudice involved in this inequality of opportunity, many are preparing students for competitive employment by setting up job experience placements for school leavers. Developing the skills outlined in Part Two of this book will also increase the ability of students to take their place within competitive employment.

The Lack of Role Models

There are very few positive role models for young people (Ward 1983). The media perpetuates images of the poor cripple, an object of pity; and the hero with a disability, the exception who made it against all odds. These images can be seen as two poles of a continuum:

Totally helpless ——————————————— Incredibly skilled

They mean little to the vast majority of disabled young people.

In order to counter these images, young people need more contact with disabled adults. The independent living movement in the United States of America developed "peer counselling services" (Saxton 1983). A peer counsellor is defined as:
". . . a disabled person who has disability related experience, knowledge and coping skills, and assists other disabled individuals with their disability related experiences" (Moses *et al.* 1982).
Peer counsellors can thus act as role models for disabled young people.

Moreover, this reinforces how essential it is that more professionals with disabilities are employed within the education system.

The Lack of Support Systems for Carers

The lack of formalised support for carers is another area of concern. Many parents find it difficult to help their able-bodied adolescents to become more independent, eg. allowing them to take risks. Enabling young people to become more independent can be even more difficult, given the extra stresses of having a disabled child and the environmental and attitudinal barriers outlined above. Somewhat paradoxically, it is often less stressful for parents to provide total care than to help teach their children to become more independent. Involving parents in programmes offered at schools, helping them to develop their own social support networks and coping styles have been found to be effective in enabling them to become less stressed and consequently more supportive of their children's fight for independence (see page **153**).

INDIVIDUALS

The above obstacles set the context within which disabled young people and those working with them are striving towards independence. However, each young person is different and an individual, and thus will experience these obstacles in different ways, at different times in their lives. Whilst it is impossible to put all young people with disabilities under the same umbrella without over-generalising, it is hoped that many of the points made in this book will be relevant to many young people.

THE HOLOGRAPHIC MODEL OF LIVING SKILLS

The overall structure for developing living skills outlined in this book, can be applied to many young people, particularly those with disabilities. This structure, namely The Holographic Model of Living Skills has been adapted from The Holographic Model of Lifeskills developed by Barry Hopson and Mike Scally (1987b). The model, which is outlined in depth in Chapter Three, is based on the concept of a hologram.

What is a Hologram?

In 1947, Dennis Gabor further developed the concept of photographing objects so that one could see the whole image in three rather than two dimensions. In 1963, this theory was put into practice and the first holographic (three dimensional) image was produced. It is now in general use as can be seen from many cheque and credit cards which contain holograms. The holographic image is useful for a living skills model: each part of the hologram relates to every other part and each part in some way contains the whole image. Therefore, it encourages an appreciation of the individual as a whole person, rather than a number of distinctly separate parts.

CHAPTER TWO
Methodology of Research

INTRODUCTION

The nebulous nature of independence presents great problems for the researcher who is trying to measure it with any degree of accuracy. This issue is even more acute when trying to evaluate the effectiveness of independence training provision.

THE PURPOSE OF THE RESEARCH

We wished to find out the extent and effectiveness of skills training. Schools and local education authorities were able to provide us with data on the extent of such training, but to evaluate the effectiveness of it, we needed to get information from young people and their parents. We needed to develop an approach which gave us data on a national level, but also an approach which told us what it would be like for young people and their parents as consumers. The experience of individuals helped us understand and interpret our hard data.

In common with Denzin (1970), we have used a variety of research methods, namely:

- Postal questionnaires,
- Structured interviews,
- Documentary analysis,
- Observation.

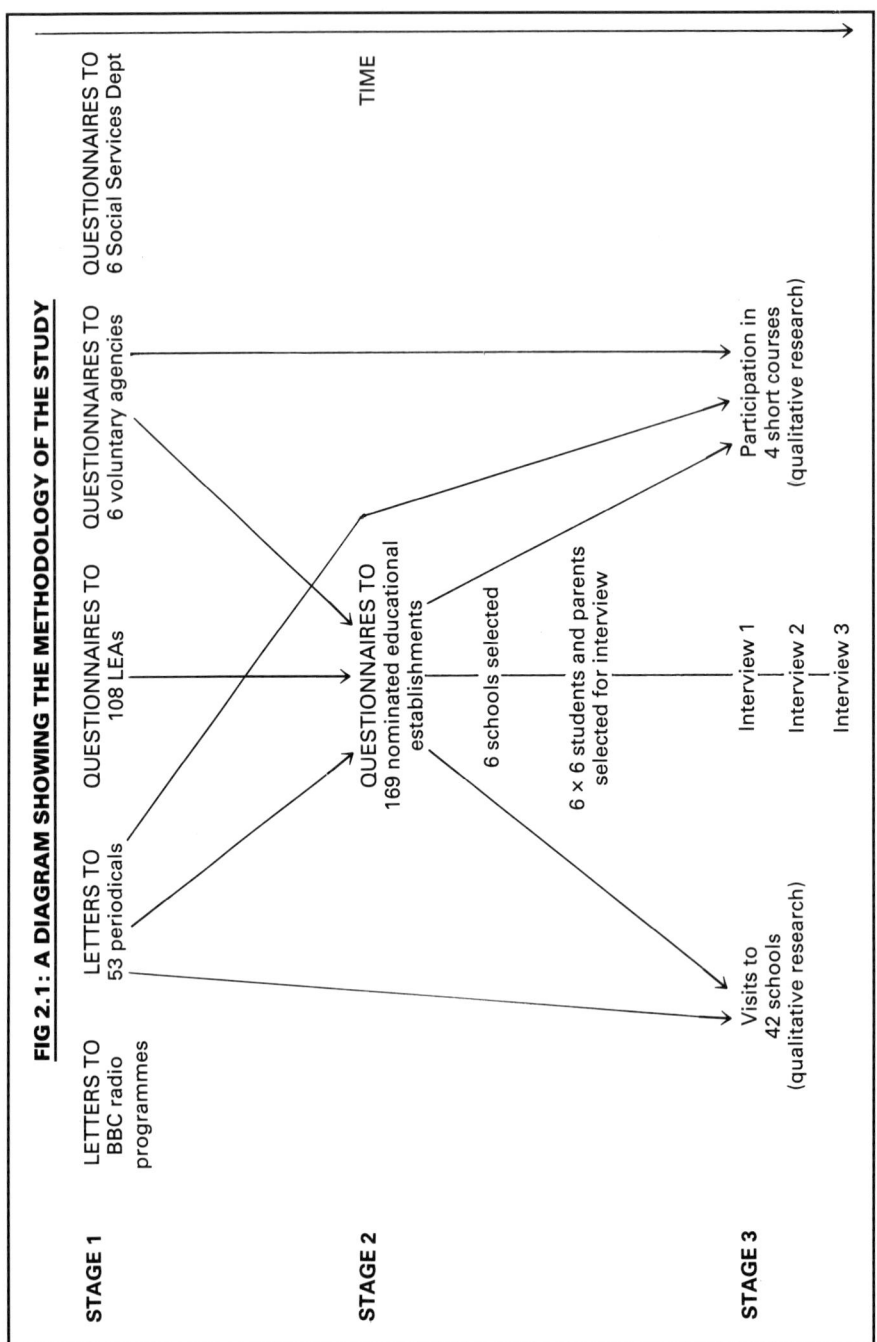

THE NATIONAL PICTURE

The first priority was to make the aims of the project known to as many individuals and organisations as possible, and to determine what training was currently available to help young people with disabilities to become more independent. A standard letter was circulated to 53 periodicals, and to producers of BBC radio programmes for people with disabilities. The letter outlined the aims of the project and invited individuals who had experience of participating in a course of "self-care and independence training", either as an administrator or consumer, to contact the researcher with their views or experiences.

This produced 22 responses, from professionals working with young people with disabilities, individuals with disabilities, people who had a member of the family with a disability, or people who had an interest in this subject.

The 108 Local Education Authorities (LEAs) in England and Wales were contacted to identify those with a policy on facilitating independence for students with disabilities in their schools. The Chief Education Officers received a brief postal questionnaire asking whether the local authority had such a policy and the names of all schools and/or colleges with the authority which were known to make this type of provision. This included ordinary schools operating policies of full integration and those with semi-segregated units and special schools with and without residential provision.

A similar questionnaire had been sent to LEAs in 1984 when RADAR began a preliminary study on developing independence in children with physical disabilities within the education system. In that instance, less than 50% of the LEAs responded to the questionnaires and it was clear that most LEAs did not regard themselves as having a policy for developing the independence of these young people.

In the present study, 54 LEAs replied initially, and a further 20 replies were received following reminders, giving a total response rate of 69%. Two years after the initial RADAR questionnaire the position seemed little changed, as few of the authorities which replied had a policy. Many stated that it was left to the schools concerned, and that it was an accepted part of the curriculum in special schools. Yet others provided a list of all the special schools in their area together with the colleges of further education, and many of these on further investigation proved not to meet the criteria of the study outlined earlier. A number of authorities stated that they had no provision for young people with physical disabilities, and that they were catered for by adjoining education authorities.

The six largest national voluntary agencies for people with disabilities which offer educational and residential provision for children were also contacted.

Details of the project were given and information was requested regarding the organisation's policy and the names and addresses of establishments offering this provision. Replies were received from all six, and authorisation given for the researchers to contact heads of the individual establishments to obtain further information. Some agencies enclosed information leaflets or documents with details of their provision. Other organisations had circulated information about the project and the request for information to their individual establishments, which resulted in invitations from heads of schools and residential units to the researcher to visit.

A standard letter was sent to the Social Services departments of six London boroughs, requesting information on their relevant provision for the identified group, and asking them to nominate establishments. Despite follow-up telephone calls, the response to these letters was poor, so it was decided not to widen the circulation to Social Services departments.

With the information received from local education authorities and voluntary organisations, a postal questionnaire was sent to 169 nominated establishments. Although only establishments within local education authorities who answered the questionnaires were contacted, the authorities which answered did cover most geographical areas within England and Wales. Schools and colleges were asked questions relating to the following factors:

- policy,
- documentation of policy or practice,
- in-service training,
- monitoring progress of students, and
- factors inhibiting independence.

The questionnaire also asked whether the establishment would be willing to accept a visit from the researcher in order to obtain further information. A total of 84 establishments replied, giving a response rate of approximately 50%, of which 69 catered for children and adolescents aged 10–16 years. The results from these 69 questionnaires are interspersed throughout the book.

EVALUATING THE TYPE OF SCHOOL PROGRAMMES

Following up the Postal Questionnaires

A checklist of key points or account agenda themes (Harre and Secord 1972) about developing independence in young people with disabilities was developed from the published and unpublished literature, and the data already obtained. Using this checklist, 42 schools were selected from those which replied to the short postal questionnaires. Each school was visited at least once, using the same checklist as a reference point (see Table 2.1 for a breakdown of the types and numbers of schools visited). We examined copies of relevant assessment, planning and monitoring tools, curriculum documents and/or policy statements where available. A detailed written account of each visit was made as soon as possible after each visit.

A small number of voluntary agencies for people with disabilities and some health authorities and schools, organise short (one to two weeks) "independence training"/"social development courses" for small groups of young people with disabilities. A sample of these courses was visited and copies of relevant documentation were again taken away and examined. The author spent some time as a volunteer on a sample of these courses and compiled detailed reports on this work.

This methodology helped gain some standardisation of enquiry, whilst allowing flexibility to note in detail fresh ideas, different approaches and adaptations to the published independence training programmes. Thus a combination of structured research involving standardised collation of data together with more detailed "impressionistic" data was usefully achieved.

TABLE 2.1: TYPES OF ESTABLISHMENTS VISITED

Type of Provision	Number of Visits
Non-maintained Special Schools (with boarding facilities)	8
LEA Special Schools (with boarding facilities)	6
LEA Special Schools (day provision)	17
LEA Ordinary Schools (with units)	4
LEA Ordinary Schools (full integration)	7
Short Courses	4
TOTAL =	46

Collating of Data

The main points from the accounts written after each visit were manually tabulated, to give a clearer picture of the current practice in facilitating independence in young people with physical disabilities. These research findings and the pertinent issues and ideas from the literature were then superimposed onto the holographic model of living skills (see page **38**).

EVALUATING THE EFFECTIVENESS OF SCHOOL PROGRAMMES

An interview schedule for young people and their parents was developed from a combination of three main sources:

- the techniques and an evaluation model developed and tested by a Research Team at the University of York Social Policy Research Unit (1982),
- assessment programmes developed by individual schools and other bodies,
- assessment schemes which are commercially available and used in schools and other institutions, including:
    Pathways to Independence (Jeffree and Cheseldine 1982)
    The New Mossford Assessment Chart (Whitehouse 1983)
    The Copewell Curriculum (Whelan, Speake and Strickland 1979)
    Transition to Adulthood (Hutchinson and Tennyson 1986)

The interview schedule was divided into five sections (Table 2.2).

TABLE 2.2: SECTIONS OF INTERVIEW SCHEDULE

Section	Topic
1	Knowledge of Impairment and Disability
2	Social and Recreational Activities
3	Activities of Daily Living
4	Mobility
5	Personal Care

A pre-interview questionnaire was designed to obtain basic classification data of the pupils to be interviewed; ie. personal information about age, sex, disability etc.

A small pilot study was carried out involving four children with disabilities who attended residential or day special schools. As the result of this, the interview schedule was revised and refined.

Six schools were chosen from those which had replied to the short postal questionnaires on the basis of their responses and the documentation enclosed. Three types of school were proposed from two distinct geographical areas (Table 2.3).

TABLE 2.3: TYPE OF SCHOOL AND GEOGRAPHICAL AREA INVOLVED IN STRUCTURED INTERVIEWS

	Ordinary School* with unit	Special School (LEA maintained)	Special School (non-maintained)
North of England	1	1	1
South of England	1	1	1

Both ordinary schools with units worked a flexible integration policy.

Nearly all of the students were fully integrated using their ordinary class and the unit as a base. Some of the students had special classes part-time and ordinary classes most of the time.

Six students aged between ten and sixteen years with primary physical impairments were selected by headteachers from each school (Tables 2.4 and 2.5). We would like to have had equal numbers of children in each cohort, but for various reasons this was not possible. The pre-interview questionnaires were completed by staff at the respective schools.

TABLE 2.4: NUMBERS OF STUDENTS IN EACH AGE RANGE

Age	Number of Students
10	2
11	6
12	5
13	8
14	8
15	6
16	1
	TOTAL = 36

TABLE 2.5: MAIN IMPAIRMENTS OF STUDENTS

Impairments	Number of Students
Spina Bifida and Hydrocephalus	10
Cerebral Palsy	12
Muscular Dystrophy	3
Others*	11
TOTAL =	36

*There was only one pupil in each category of impairment, eg. one pupil with Neuromyopathy, one with Cystic Fibrosis, one with Spinal Muscular Atrophy, etc.

Six researchers were employed to conduct the interviews in their geographical area. An interviewer's briefing day was held at RADAR which covered some basic techniques of administering structured interview schedules.

A series of three interview sessions was carried out with each student immediately before, immediately after and one term after students had participated in a section of an ongoing "independence" programme. This approach was taken to alleviate some of the inherent difficulties in evaluating the effectiveness of schools' programmes. Often self-care and independence training in schools and colleges is carried out over a number of years; a number of schools stated that it began the moment a young person first entered the school, and continued throughout the school life of that student. Some programmes were designed for school leavers, and were carried out over the final one, two or three years of a student's school career. Several schools seemed to carry out a combination of the above, followed by an intensive school leavers' preparation programme over one term of the student's final year. Yet other schools and colleges held short residential sessions for independence assessment and training of one or two weeks, as part of their overall programmes. In essence, it is very difficult to assess the impact of a course which spans a number of years, given time constraints on the research.

The same interview schedule was used for both parents and students to check accuracy of responses. It is important to emphasise that all answers to questions were opinion, not necessarily fact. Parents and young people were interviewed separately to enable respondents to disclose attitudes and feelings which could only be expressed in confidence. It was also anticipated that some parents, if interviewed with their children, might dominate the questioning and/or influence their children's responses. Each interview with a student and her parent(s) was carried out by the same independent interviewer. Since the interview schedule covered a broad spectrum of perceptions and skills, it took approximately one and a half hours to complete. Some young people were unable to maintain concentration and so were interviewed in two separate sessions. Additional information was obtained from the schools involved by discussions with school staff and with reference to school records.

The data obtained from the interview schedule was analysed by computer using the Statistical Package for the Social Sciences. The results obtained are interspersed throughout the book.

THE SUBJECTS OF THE RESEARCH

The Age Range

Time and financial constraints made it necessary to narrow the age range so that the process of facilitating independence in one group could be investigated in depth, ie. physical, social, psychological and political aspects. After extensive consultation it was decided to focus on those aged 10–16 years. Research conducted with the 16–19 age group, the school leavers, suggest that many young people in this age group need extra help as they adjust to adult expectations and adult life (eg. Hutchinson and Tennyson 1986; Thomas *et al*. 1987). However, at this age there is a danger that intervention becomes remedial. Furthermore, at such a late stage it may be more difficult to learn new skills as this may involve unlearning old inappropriate patterns. For example, someone who has never made a bed at 16 years old, has both to learn the skills of making beds and unlearn the expectation that others will make it. Therefore, more intervention is needed at an earlier age.

There seem to be few studies investigating the beginning of the process of facilitating independence for children under ten years old. Portage and other schemes focused some training on self-care skills and the partnership between parents and professionals (Dessent 1984), but the 10–16 year "gap" became apparent. It seemed particularly useful to focus on this potentially very fruitful age range as first, a sense of self starts to be crystallised at about 10 years old and secondly, young people are gaining more independence between the ages of 10 and 16 as they progress through adolescence.

Range of Impairments

This study attempts to consider those young people with primarily physical impairments. Studies have shown that there is considerable overlap between young people with intellectual and physical impairments, which must be recognised (Anderson 1982). The trend towards integration of students with disabilities into ordinary schools following the Education Act 1981, has led to a shift in population within ordinary and special schools. Many special schools, originally intended for those with physical impairments, now have students with both severe physical disabilities and learning difficulties. Thus, it is necessary for this book to consider young people with physical and secondary intellectual impairments if it is to reflect reality in today's schools. Young people with primarily physical impairments (eg. Spina Bifida, Cerebral Palsy) make up the largest groups in this study while those with secondary learning difficulties (eg. Hydrocephalus) are also considered. The book is biased towards young people who use wheelchairs.

Issues specifically related to young people with progressive conditions (eg. Duchenne Muscular Dystrophy) are considered briefly, but those with severe learning difficulties and those with sensory impairments are beyond the scope of this book.

Ethnic Minorities

This book aims to suggest some of the differences involved in working with children with disabilities from ethnic minorities, but does not attempt to deal with the issues as there is very little research in this area (Nathwani and Perkins 1987).

SUMMARY

We investigated the extent and effectiveness of programmes which help young people with disabilities to become more independent. We used quantitative and qualitative research techniques to gain a clear picture of these programmes. The study results published in this book stem from five main sources:

1. Responses to postal questionnaires sent to educational establishments.

2. Detailed reports of visits to schools.

3. Detailed reports of short "Independence Training" courses.

4. Analysis of documentation on policy or practice from long-term schools programmes, short courses and other "independence training" programmes.

5. Structured interviews conducted with young people with disabilities and their families

These results are interspersed throughout this book.

CHAPTER THREE
A Holographic Model of Living Skills

This research study shows that schools use different approaches to enable young people with disabilities to become more independent. When visiting schools, the researcher was frequently told that developing independence was the general school ethos, thus explicit "independence" lessons did not need to be timetabled. However, when staff were asked for more details, many were unable to state the specific process and goals. Although it is unwise to view "independence" as just one of many timetabled lessons, there is a danger that the general approach can lead to a substantial gap between theory and practice.

Some schools supplemented their general approach by using the short "self-care and independence training" courses currently offered by some special schools, hospitals and the voluntary sector. These courses are particularly useful for assessment purposes. However, it is unlikely that the short-time period can effectively enable young people to do more than learn the techniques of specific skills, which will require practice over a longer period so that they may become more independent on a long-term basis. Other schools used these short-courses to reinforce weekly "self-care and independence training" lessons, sometimes timetabled under the auspices of a living skills curriculum. These courses usually worked from the principles of behaviour modification using task analysis as the main assessment and teaching tool.

TABLE 3.1: FACTORS WHICH INHIBIT INDEPENDENCE

Factors stated by staff	Number of responses from schools
Internal factors	
Passivity	9
Poor self-image/lacking self-confidence	10
Lack of motivation	16
Expectation that others should help	6
Embarrassment	2
Poor concentration	8
Physical impairment itself	8
Low intellectual ability	13
Incontinence	6
School factors	
Limited life experience	7
Overprotection by peers	4
Overprotection by adults, eg. non-teaching assistants, parents	28
Low expectations from adults	17
Shortage of occupational therapy	1*
Lack of residential facilities in school	8
Lack of accessibility to all facilities	3
Fragmented training programmes – not prioritised	10
Training not started early enough	5
Poor parent–school liaison	3
High adult–pupil ratio in school	1
Societal factors	
Society's attitudes	5
Lack of accessibility to community	12
Inappropriate living conditions	9
Lack of aids in the home	7
Familial factors	
Parental concern	32
Parental need for a dependent child	8
Lack of community support facilities for families	1
Time factor	
Lack of time	19
Not applicable	4*

*All responses were from ordinary schools.

Both the short courses and the timetabled curricula examined in this study were developed within the "fix-it" model of independence. Within this philosophy, young people with disabilities are encouraged to strive for the able-bodied norm by completing physical tasks without assistance (see page **18**). It is argued that while these courses may have their place within the curriculum, they do not go far enough. It is not necessarily helpful to press for physical independence if young people are too psychologically afraid to use it. For example, an individual may have the skills to make a cup of coffee without any assistance, but may not have the confidence to use those skills without someone watching her.

The postal questionnaires sent to schools revealed, in answer to an open-ended question, that staff perceived many of the inhibiting factors to the development of even self-care skills as being primarily psychological in nature (Table 3.1). For example, poor self-image, lack of confidence and motivation were seen by many professionals as inhibiting factors.

Although these issues were acknowledged by professionals inside and outside the education system, they were rarely systematically addressed within the models of working towards independence within schools. To some extent, the aims of teaching young people with disabilities to complete physical tasks without assistance, has been achieved. The emphasis has enabled many young people to develop self-care skills, so becoming less dependent on service providers. It is because of this work, pioneered within special schools and the voluntary sector, that it is now realistic to move on to a wider model of developing independence.

The recent developments in Personal and Social Education (PSE) and Personal Social Moral Education (PSME) within ordinary schools have also contributed to the groundwork for this model. The majority of ordinary and some special schools visited in this study, timetabled Personal and Social Education. These courses address wide personal, social and moral issues and often aim at improving young people's confidence and self-image. However, some have argued that timetabling this subject is a strategy for trivialising personal and social development, as it should be at the heart of all education (Pring 1987). This aside, within ordinary schools these courses rarely addressed disability issues, and within all schools, the courses were rarely systematically linked with any "self-care and independence training" offered. Thus, even in schools where the many facets of independence were addressed somewhere within the curriculum, the approach tended to lack cohesion.

The Holographic Model of Lifeskills was initially developed for use with 15–16 year old able-bodied young British people (Hopson and Scally 1987b). It is also meaningful for the development of children and adults. The methods of delivery and specific course content may differ, but the essential principles apply to all age groups. The term "life skills" has connotations of skills for the future, whereas "living skills" is as applicable to the present and takes account of the needs of young people with progressive conditions. Thus, the title of the model has been slightly changed for use in this study. Otherwise, their model will be used stressing the aspects particularly pertinent to young people with physical disabilities between the ages of 12–16 years, and in less detail, the use of the model with respect to the development of professionals and parents.

THE ASPECTS OF THE HOLOGRAPHIC MODEL OF LIVING SKILLS

The idea of the hologram was adopted to incorporate the elements shown in Fig 3.1. The model of living skills looks like a 12-sided figure (dodecahedron) when drawn on paper. The most important points to remember are:

1. The objective of the model of living skills is to enable young people to develop physical, intellectual and emotional independence.
2. Every aspect of the model relates to every other and each must be seen as part of the whole.
3. Every aspect of the model is as important as every other.

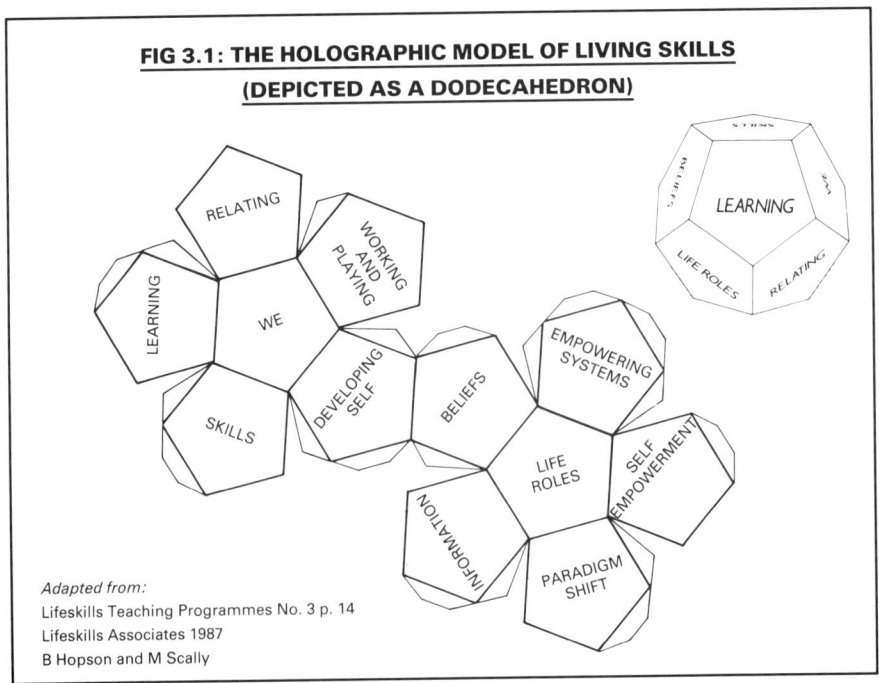

FIG 3.1: THE HOLOGRAPHIC MODEL OF LIVING SKILLS (DEPICTED AS A DODECAHEDRON)

Adapted from:
Lifeskills Teaching Programmes No. 3 p. 14
Lifeskills Associates 1987
B Hopson and M Scally

There are a number of different ways to describe the model in one sentence. The following summary identifies one main strand of the model before it is explained in more detail:

WE (1) need to understand and act upon our **BELIEFS** (2), have **INFORMATION** (3) and the **SKILLS** (4) including **DEVELOPING SELF** (5), **LEARNING** (6), **RELATING** (7) and **WORKING AND PLAYING** (8) in order to become more **SELF-EMPOWERED** (9) and to form **EMPOWERING SYSTEMS** (10) and appropriately fulfil our **LIFE ROLES** (11) in a dynamic environment (**PARADIGM SHIFT** (12)).

(1) **WE**

"We" refers to the individual and group of individuals interested in using the model to become more independent.

(2) **BELIEFS**

We each hold a set of beliefs which are the fundamental premise from which we operate. They need to be stated for us to understand the ways in which they influence the way we live and work. Beliefs are not static and must be restated as changes occur. The beliefs upon which this book is based were outlined at the beginning of Chapter One (see page **19**).

(3) **INFORMATION**

This aspect of the model is infinite in size. Information can be divided into **information about the self, information about others** and **information about the system**. Information enables us to obtain, retain and use power (see page **77**).

(4) **SKILLS**

The model identifies four groups of skills, all of which are interrelated and equally important. These groupings have been slightly adapted from Lifeskills Teaching Programmes No. 4 (Hopson and Scally 1987c), identifying specific skills pertinent to young people with disabilities (see Fig 3.2). The list is not exhaustive and will be adapted to meet the needs of students in each school. These four main groups of skills are examined in greater depth in Part Two of this book. Chapter Five explores **"DEVELOPING SELF"** (5), Chapter Six looks at some of the skills of **"LEARNING"** (6), Chapter Seven at **"RELATING"** (7) and Chapter Eight at **"WORKING AND PLAYING"** (8).

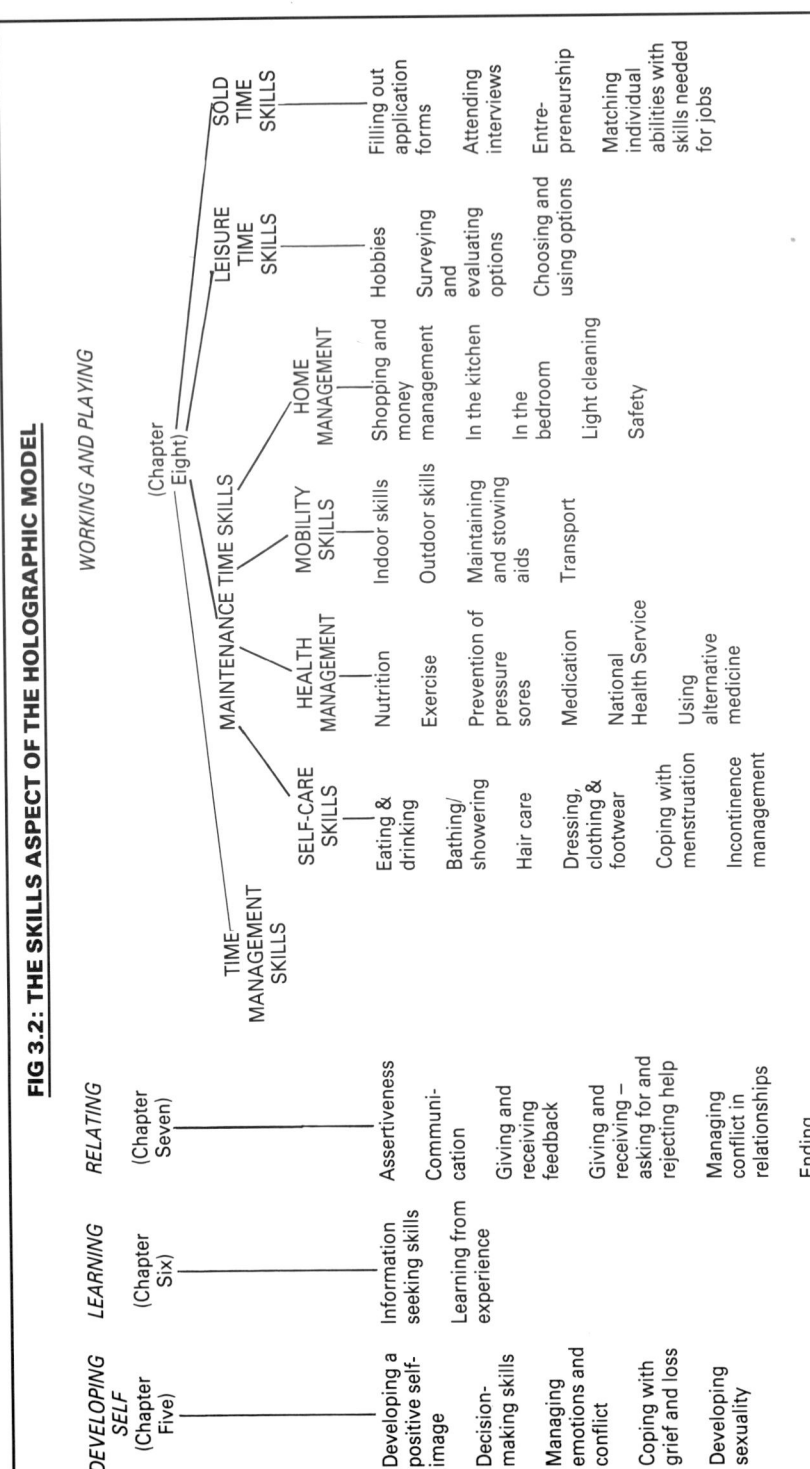

(9) **SELF-EMPOWERMENT**

Self-empowerment is the process of becoming more in control of oneself and one's life (see Chapter Four).

(10) **EMPOWERING SYSTEMS**

An empowering system is open to change, pro-active and sufficiently supportive and flexible to meet individual needs (see Chapter Four).

(11) **LIFE ROLES**

We undertake a number of different roles throughout life (see Fig 3.3). Each role leads to a difference in the way we relate and are related to (see Chapter Seven).

FIG 3.3: LIFE ROLES

LEARNER

WORKER

PARTNER

FRIEND

PARENT

CHILD

HOMEMAKER

LEISURE USER

CITIZEN

CONSUMER*

*This includes being an active consumer of services offered to young people with disabilities, eg. physiotherapy, occupational therapy, medicine.

---

(12) **PARADIGM SHIFT**

The model identifies a paradigm shift from the past industrial era to the future information era. A major cause of stress within society is the tremendous rate of change due to rapid advances in information technology. This aspect of the model attempts to pinpoint some of these associated changes. These changes are outside the scope of this book (Appendix 3).

Having outlined the holographic model of living skills, we will now explore the concept of empowerment in greater depth.

CHAPTER FOUR
Empowerment

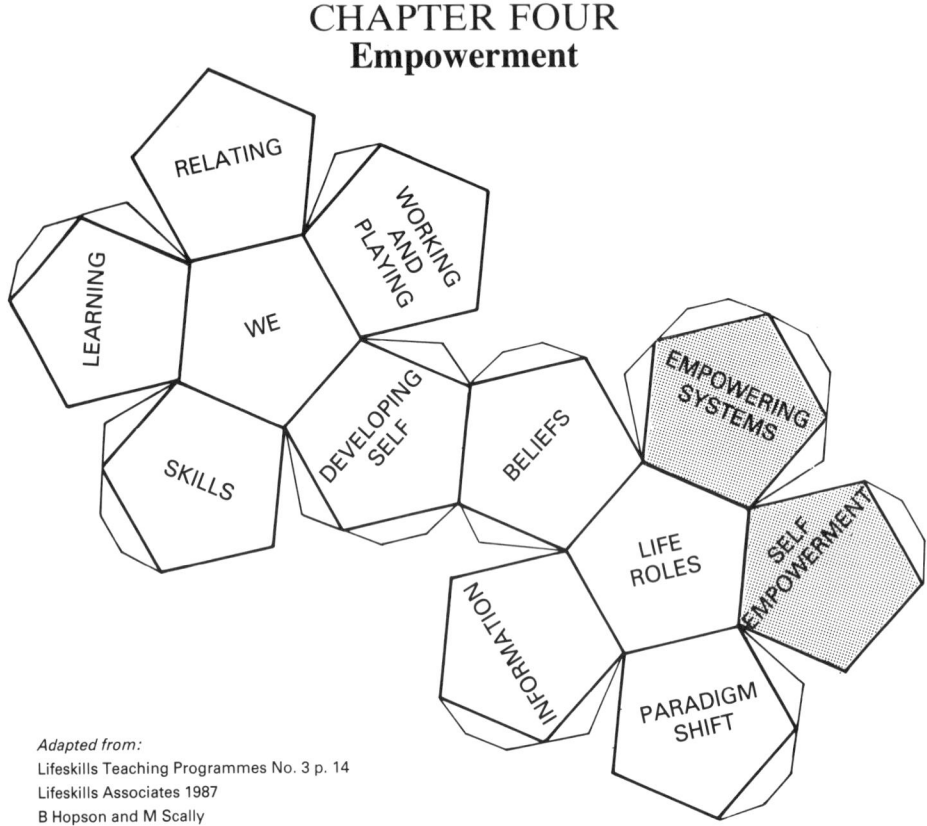

Adapted from:
Lifeskills Teaching Programmes No. 3 p. 14
Lifeskills Associates 1987
B Hopson and M Scally

Empowerment and the holographic model of living skills are inextricably intertwined. It is essential to understand the concept of empowerment for the holographic model of living skills to be used to its best effect, and since empowerment may be a new concept to some, it needs to be more fully explained. The key to understanding empowerment is an understanding of the notion of self-empowerment.

Self-empowerment is a process of becoming increasingly more in control of oneself and one's life, and thus increasingly more independent.

Self-empowerment is a means by which an individual can draw on her individual inner strengths and resources. Everyone can become more self-empowered – professionals, students with disabilities and their parents. The more self-empowered an individual becomes, the more she will be able to help bring out this process in others, so if a professional feels more self-empowered, she will be in a better position to enable those with whom she is working to develop.

The following dimensions help to differentiate between more and less self-empowered individuals (Fig 4.1).

FIG 4.1: DIFFERENTIATION BETWEEN A MORE OR LESS SELF-EMPOWERED PERSON

More Self-Empowered	*Less Self-Empowered*
Pro-active	Reactive
Open to change	Closed to change
Assertive	Non-assertive or aggressive
Self-accountable	Blames others
Self-directed	Other-directed
Uses feelings	Overwhelmed by or fails to recognise feelings
Learns from mistakes	Debilitated by mistakes
Confronts	Avoids
Lives more in the present	Past- or future-orientated
Realistic	Unrealistic
Thinks relatively	Thinks in absolutes
Seeks alternatives	Tunnel vision
Develops commitments	Keeps obligations
Likes self	Dislikes self
Values others	Negates others
Alert to others' needs	Selfish
Interested in the world	Self-centred
Balanced life-style	One arena of life developed to the exclusion of others
Enhances other people's lives	Restricts the lives of others
Takes control	Assumes others are experts

Reproduced from:
Lifeskills Teaching (p. 58)
B Hopson and M Scally
McGraw-Hill 1981

Taken together, these generalised points offer helpful insights into the notion of self-empowerment. Hopson and Scally (1981c) also help clarify the meaning of self-empowerment by using the analogy of a pinball machine to illustrate the antithesis of living in this way:

> "Balls in a pinball machine have no life of their own; they are set in motion by someone else and then bounce from one place to another without any clear direction, sometimes even making big scores, but then sinking into oblivion until someone sets them off again."

Clearly "pinball living" is reactive. The process of self-empowerment equips people to live a more pro-active life. All of us live somewhat reactively as we can never be immune to external influences. Education towards self-empowerment endeavours to tip the balance in favour of pro-activity wherever possible, whilst taking into account the possible effects of the social and attitudinal barriers outlined in Chapter One.

Awareness is the primary prerequisite for self-empowerment as well as the beginning of the process towards it. For the sake of clarity, the notion of awareness has been subdivided into self-awareness, awareness of others and awareness of the system.

Self-awareness is defined as becoming conscious of and listening to one's emotions and innermost thoughts. It involves a knowledge of one's strengths, limitations and potential. Self-awareness also reflects increased understanding of the way one affects and is perceived by others. Awareness of others stems from self-awareness and involves sensitivity towards others. It is also a criteria for self-empowered behaviour.

Self-awareness and awareness of others can be heightened by an understanding of the way one influences and is influenced by society's social structures and environment, ie. awareness of the system.

To translate the holographic model and the inter-linked notion of self-empowerment into everyday practice, it is helpful to identify specific goals of things one wants to change within oneself and/or within the system. Commitment to these goals arises from the options available. The outcomes of these goals should be specified so that each individual knows what she is trying to achieve. The goals chosen are likely to reflect the beliefs of the individual or system. Beliefs play an essential part in the educative process.

Awareness, goals, beliefs, living skills and information have been identified as the fundamentals of self-empowered behaviour (Fig 4.2). These form a working definition of self-empowerment for everyone and are the major features of the holographic model of living skills.

FIG 4.2: FUNDAMENTALS OF SELF-EMPOWERED BEHAVIOUR

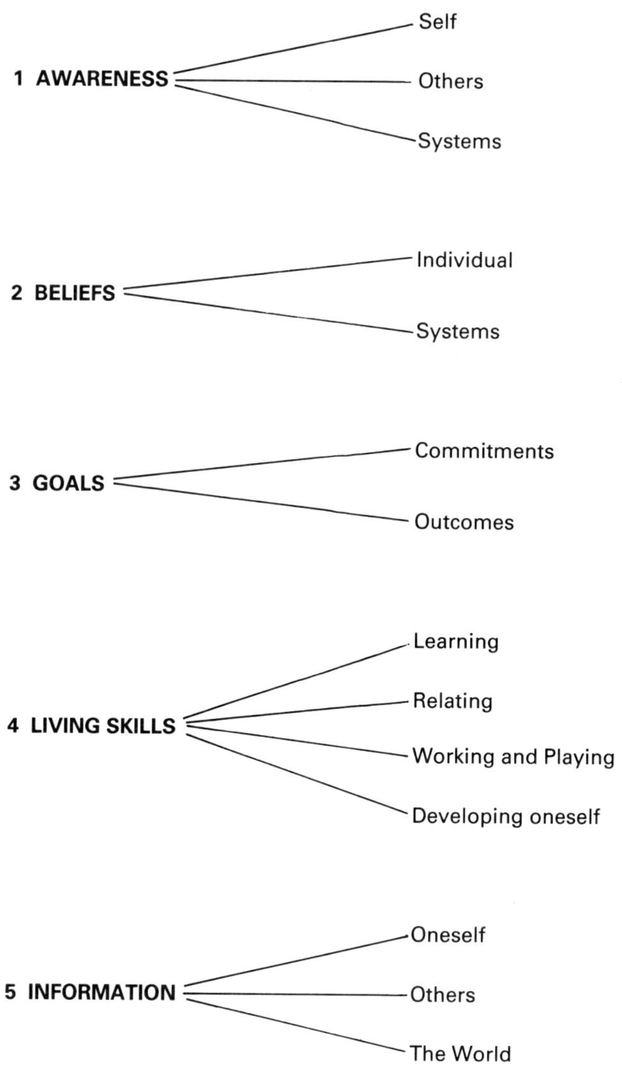

1 AWARENESS
- Self
- Others
- Systems

2 BELIEFS
- Individual
- Systems

3 GOALS
- Commitments
- Outcomes

4 LIVING SKILLS
- Learning
- Relating
- Working and Playing
- Developing oneself

5 INFORMATION
- Oneself
- Others
- The World

Adapted from:
Lifeskills Teaching (p. 59)
B Hopson and M Scally
McGraw-Hill 1981

Having considered the notion of self-empowerment, it is useful to see how this relates to an empowering system.

An empowering system is open to change, pro-active, self-accountable and sufficiently supportive and flexible to meet individual needs.

As such, it is impossible to define in a static and compartmentalised manner. An empowering education system enables students, parents, professionals and ancillary staff to grow and develop by actively encouraging attitudes and behaviours which reflect sensitivity and respect. It relies on honest relations between everyone.

An interactive relationship exists between an empowering system and the individuals that work in and use that system.

Self-empowered ⇌ Empowering
Individuals   System

If the general system encourages the individual to develop, her input will increase the capacity of the system to encourage more individual growth and development. Some suggestions on how to develop an empowering system are made in the final part of the book. A number of the issues of self-empowerment for professionals will now be examined in relation to awareness, beliefs, goals, skills and information.

SELF-EMPOWERMENT AND PROFESSIONALS

1. AWARENESS

It is important for professionals to be aware of the many factors which influence them and thus, directly or indirectly, the young people with whom they work. Professionals are not immune to the same societal messages which affect young people with disabilities and their parents, eg. religious codes, social and political pressures and the taboos of sex and of death.

Working with young people with disabilities can be difficult. For example, it can be distressing or frightening to be with people you may perceive as being trapped in a deformed or uncontrollable body. Because of this, you may be tempted to do things for them so that they can feel cared for and comforted, and as compensation, for their lives to be made easier. To some extent, this also helps to avoid the pain and fear you may associate with becoming disabled yourself.

Likewise, when working with young people with progressive conditions, you are likely to need to develop strong defence mechanisms which help you to cope with impending death. An awareness and knowledge of these defences may be helpful (eg. denial and projection). Professionals are not immune to reactions of shock and grief (Wolff 1974). Many of those who participated in this study seemed to deny these reactions, rather than sharing and working through them with each other. This not only contributes to their high levels of stress, but also makes it more difficult for them to enable young people with deteriorating conditions and their peers to come to terms with their grief (Liddell 1982).

It may be helpful if schools set up staff development workshops to explore these issues. In these workshops, staff could reflect on the ways in which they empower and depower students with disabilities at both the staff team level and the institutional level, and how they themselves are empowered and depowered by each other, the school and wider education system. Appendix 4 may be a useful starting point for discussion (see page **192**).

2. BELIEFS

An empowering belief system is an important prerequisite to helping young people with disabilities to develop their independence. It is desirable for professionals to attempt to clarify their own belief systems from which they work with young people with disabilities, as these beliefs will directly influence their practice (see page **19**). It is also useful if the staff team identify the beliefs on which the staff team and the school operates. These will partially reflect the attitudes of the head teacher, and the philosophy of the Local Education Authority or the voluntary agency running the school. Staff development workshops could be an ideal forum to examine the implications of these beliefs on policy, practice and the everyday workings of the school.

3. GOALS

Enabling young people with disabilities to become more independent is the broad objective, but genuine, determined commitment to this well-intentioned objective is needed if it is to become a reality. It is therefore important to break down this aim into definable goals, eg. staff can assist students and their parents to state a number of specific objectives towards which they want to work.

With greater self-awareness, an individual member of staff may also wish to change some of the ways in which she works to become more empowering to students. This goal is so broad that it could lead to no change at all as it is very difficult to change well-established patterns. Therefore, it may be more realistic if she identifies her own clearly defined objectives. When visiting schools, the researchers in the study frequently heard staff talk about young people as their impairments, eg. the "spastics", "the spina bifs", the "MDs". This gives the impression that the individuals behind the labels are not seen.

Thus, one such objective could be to refrain from referring to young people in terms of their impairments. Setting meaningful individual objectives can be facilitated through effective supervision (see page **145**).

4. SKILLS

Staff need skills in two main inter-connected categories:
- general skills for living, and
- skills for the individual's role.

The former category of skills is the same as those featured in the student curriculum (see Part Two). For example, the skills of time-management, communication, maintaining relationships, assertiveness and management of emotions and conflict, could all usefully be considered within staff training. This has two functions: the acquisition of the skills and the first-hand experience of the content and methodology of this work (Anderson 1988).

The latter category of skills refers to the individual's particular professional role in the educational environment, eg. skills of occupational therapy, skills of care work (see page **151**).

5. INFORMATION

This fundamental of self-empowerment is all-embracing. It relates to knowledge about your own strengths, limitations and potential, information about other staff's roles and the young people with whom you are working, and information about the education system and other organisations providing services to young people with disabilities.

Information about oneself can come from feedback during staff development workshops and individual supervision sessions, if available. Information about students with disabilities can be accurately passed to staff at regular staff meetings, given a fundamental commitment from all team members to communication. If individuals from each discipline make active attempts to translate their professional jargon into common language, this would help to break down the barriers to interdisciplinary work (see page **139**).

It is important for professionals to apply these fundamentals of self-empowerment to themselves, before and at the same time as facilitating this process in others. The issues outlined in this section are not exclusively pertinent to professionals. In most instances, parents could be substituted for professionals, so providing a starting point for parent workshops (see page **159**). The needs and specific types of provision will be different for parents and professionals but the care issues will be the same. Central to the notion of self-empowerment is the recognition of individual needs and the importance of all those involved having the opportunity to develop their own goals, so strengthening their commitment to them.

SELF-EMPOWERMENT AND THE ADVOCACY MOVEMENT

In recent times, an advocacy movement has grown amongst adults with physical disabilities and/or learning difficulties, and has affected and been affected by their raised expectations and the wider range of opportunities available to them.

Self-advocates are speaking out and becoming more self-confident, assertive and independent. They are collectively challenging the oppression they feel they have suffered from the public and professionals alike (Statham 1987). When individuals do not feel sufficiently confident and skilled to speak up for themselves, or if they think that their views will not be taken seriously, they sometimes enlist the help of an advocate. The advocate's role is to represent the interests of the individual concerned, as defined and stated by that individual. The role of advocate is equivalent to the role of facilitator; however, whereas advocates offer individuals the benefits of cognitive and psycho-social skills, facilitators offer enabling physical skills. Both advocates and facilitators enable the individual concerned to take more control over her own life.

If an individual feels depowered, however, she is likely to find it difficult to take on this control. It is argued that self-empowerment is both a prerequisite to and the process which can enable young people with physical disabilities and/or learning difficulties to benefit most from the advocacy movement. Unless an individual is more self-empowered, she will be unable to effectively advocate for herself and/or use an advocate to her best advantage.

In essence, advocacy skills are the same as those which enable an individual to become more self-empowered. Although the benefits of adults developing these skills are widely documented (eg. Hersov and Cooper 1986), there is still little research within the advocacy movement relating to the development of these skills in younger people with disabilities within schools. One exception is an evaluative study of an advocacy skills curriculum, which found that there were benefits for students, their parents and professionals who became more aware of both individual student's potential and disability issues (Razeghi *et al.* 1983).

Having discussed the concept of empowerment, we can now go on to look at the skills facet of the holographic model. These skills could be developed under the auspices of an advocacy curriculum.

PART TWO

Skills

CHAPTER FIVE
Developing Self

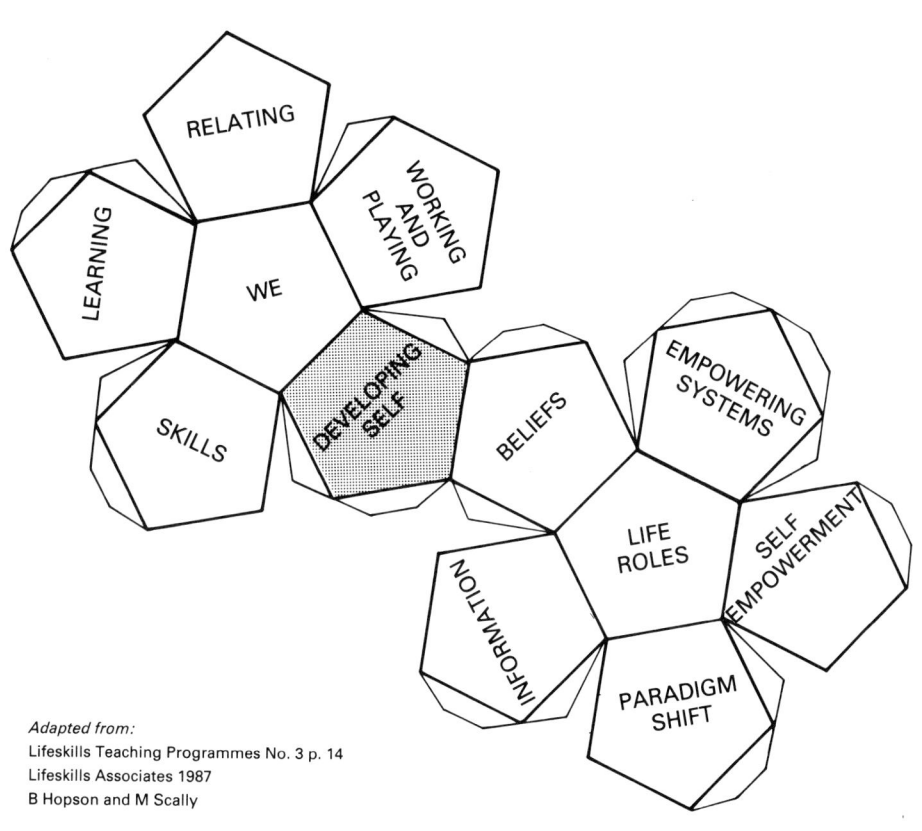

Adapted from:
Lifeskills Teaching Programmes No. 3 p. 14
Lifeskills Associates 1987
B Hopson and M Scally

This chapter focuses on the major issues involved in empowering young people with disabilities. The skills involved in self-development generally relate to feelings, emotions and thoughts. Acquiring these skills and addressing these somewhat abstract issues underpins the ability to aquire other skills. All of us need to feel more positive about ourselves to be able to make decisions, to manage our emotions and to develop our sexuality. It is often assumed that young people will develop these aspects of self-empowered behaviour without direct intervention, as a by-product of the education process. However, there is little evidence to support this assumption and these skills can and should be developed explicitly through the "Living Skills Curriculum".

DEVELOPING A POSITIVE SELF-IMAGE

The development of a positive self-image underlies all learning and is an essential aspect of education. This study shows that many staff in educational establishments see "negative self-image" as an inhibiting factor to young people becoming more independent in their self-care (Table 3.1). One of the ways to counteract a negative self-image is to make time within the curriculum to focus on the development of self-esteem, and to address the issues particularly pertinent to young people with disabilities. This section considers some of the forms this can take.

It is generally accepted that role-modelling is an important part of the learning process and that professionals in schools act as role models for students. Since role models are most effective if they have attributes similar to those of the observers (Bandura 1977), it is argued that students with visible disabilities need positive role models with visible disabilities. If a disabled adult is introduced specifically for this purpose, it is important that schools give her a clear, thorough briefing session outlining her role. Otherwise, there is a danger that she will portray her life history as typical of all people with disabilities, which may give false expectations to some students.

Ideally, professionals with disabilities should be employed in key roles within the school. However, research evidence indicates, for example, that local education authorities do not always adapt to meet the needs of teachers with disabilities and that many have experienced considerable discrimination when applying for posts (Kettle 1986). In the short term, if it is not possible to employ more professionals with disabilities, it would be helpful to involve other adults with disabilities in various classes. Role models are particularly important as many young people do not have opportunities to meet empowered adults with disabilities.

Furthermore, there is anecdotal evidence to suggest that some never meet any disabled adults, and this may lead to a belief that their physical impairments are temporary; a belief that is reinforced by the marked absence of disabled adults on "peak-time" television and "general release" cinema. The realisation that their impairments are permanent may be devastating for some young people, so this needs to be addressed very sensitively. The art department at one inner-London school made puppets with disabilities and asked a writer with a disability to make up a story around the puppets (Fig 5.1). By giving people with disabilities a high profile in art, students were reported to feel more important and valued and slightly more self-confident after the exercise.

FIG 5.1: MR AND MRS WHEELY

FIG 5.2: PAINTING

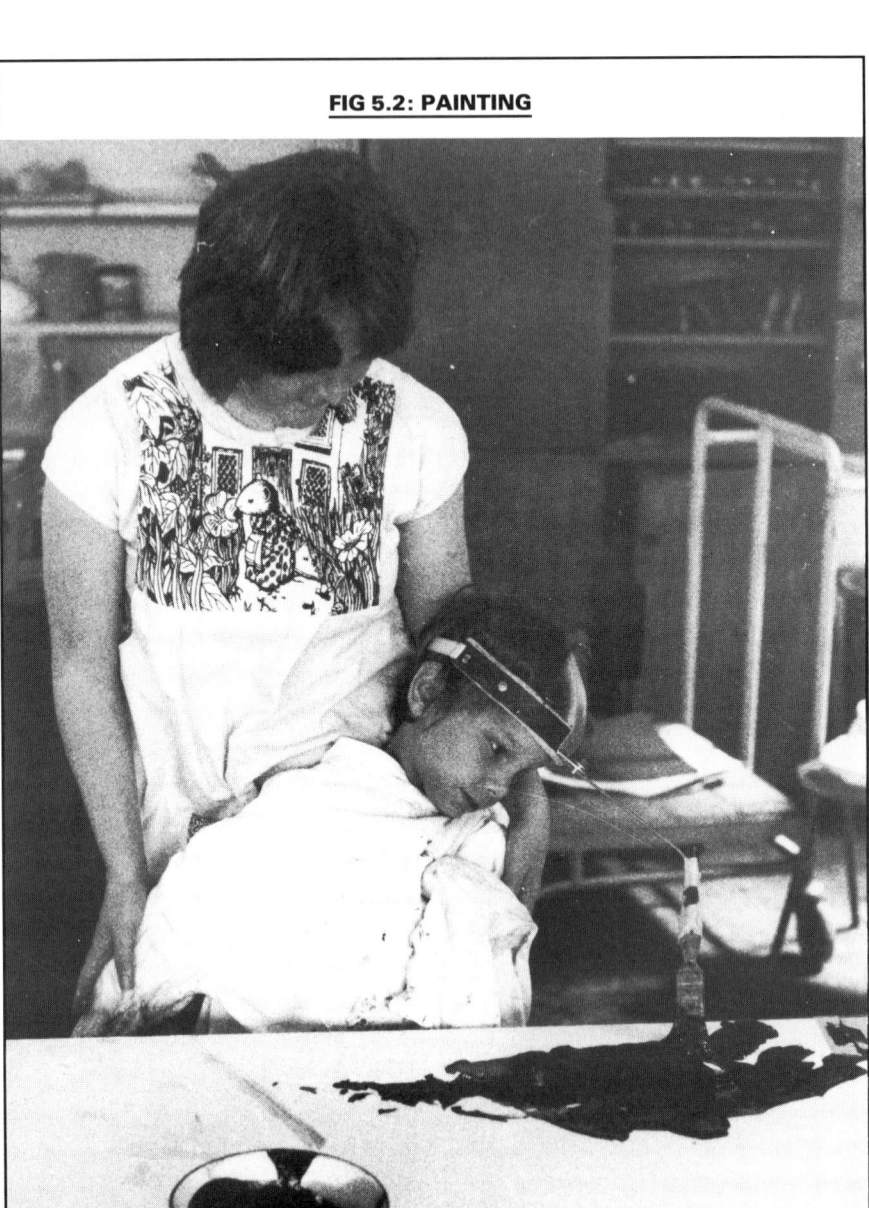

It is much more difficult for young people with severely restricted mobility or/and involuntary movements, to act directly on their environment, to write, paint, draw or play sports. If at all possible, schools should ensure that young people are given the opportunity physically to create something, as this is likely to promote self-confidence and self-esteem. The art department mentioned made a simple head device that enabled one boy to paint a picture which was later displayed on a classroom wall (Fig 5.2).

Body image, the mental representation of one's own body is an integral part of self-image. Some research evidence has found that people with physical disabilities describe themselves in more negative terms than do able-bodied people (eg. Fairchild 1976), which supports the assumption that people with disabilities have more negative images of themselves. The presence of physical disability has been associated with poor self-esteem, greater anxiety and a less-integrated perception of self (Harvey and Greenway 1984). On the other hand, there is also considerable research evidence to question the validity of this assumption. Wright (1960) concluded that there was little research evidence to suggest that particular types of physical disability are associated with specific personality characteristics, for instance self-esteem – a conclusion that is still valid today. It is argued that, although many people's self-image may be threatened by physical disability, an individual's perception of her disability is far more important than the actual impairment: everyone, able-bodied and disabled alike, is likely to feel inferior about some of her attributes. For example, the media portrayal of the "perfect" female body has had a damaging effect on the self-esteem of many women whose bodies do not fit the stereotype (Orbach 1978). It is not surprising therefore that many adolescent girls with visible disabilities tend to have negative body-images, especially as adolescence is a period when acceptance by peers, conformity to peer pressure, independence from family ties and an acute awareness of physique are particularly highlighted.

The curriculum should include a critical examination of the portrayal within the media of women, men and adolescents both able-bodied and with disabilities. The use of various mediums such as making collages of pictures cut out from newspapers and magazines can act as a starting point for discussion on the effects of this imagery on young people and how realistic these images are. However, aside from images in charitable advertisements, there are very few pictures of people with disabilities in the media, which is in itself indicative of society's attitude towards disability. When pictures are found, the polarised imagery quickly becomes apparent: people with disabilities are generally portrayed as heroic or pathetic. This stereotyped imagery is just as pronounced in literature, so extracts from books can be equally effective starting points for discussion eg. Clara in "Heidi" is portrayed as the pathetic invalid. These are examples of sexual and disability stereotypes.

Promoting discussions about body image and self-esteem in a general sense can lead to an exploration of these concepts both specific to disability and on a more personal level. Self-expression through art and drama can enable young people to focus on how they perceive their bodies, for example, through guided fantasies, movement and relaxation training (Wooster *et al.* 1986). Facial expressions and body movement can be explored through basic mirroring exercises and the actual use of mirrors.

Through art and drama therapy, young people can express feelings and thoughts about themselves which cause anxiety. If the anxieties are recognised and expressed, they are likely to be easier to address. However, people working with young people at this level need appropriate training, otherwise the open expression of feelings can be terrifying and counter-productive.

Raising the issues relating to self-image and body image as related to disability can enable young people with disabilities to explore their other positive and negative attributes, and vice versa. If young people have a basic confidence in themselves, they can afford to be more open to accepting or changing where possible those aspects which they find more difficult to accept and more limiting.

DECISION MAKING

The ability to make decisions involves the recognition of choice and the experience that your decisions count. Choices range from the most basic (eg. deciding what to eat or wear) to the more complex (eg. deciding what to do on leaving school). By learning decision-making skills and determining some choices on their own, young people will become more self-empowered, believing they have the right, the need, the will and the skills to make decisions for themselves (McTaggart and Gould 1988). It has been argued that even decisions as serious as whether to have an operation, can be vested in most young people when they have enough information from experienced adults (Deatrick 1984).

The present study shows that staff within educational establishments consider passivity to be one of the inhibiting factors to independence (Table 3.1). Passivity encourages other people to take control and thus is a way of avoiding making decisions. It is not surprising that many young people with disabilities display passive behaviours if they are surrounded by many "experts" and always have since babyhood. It is argued that schools should compensate for this "education in passivity", by teaching decision-making skills and providing additional opportunities for young people to practise these skills.

The skills of decision-making involve choosing a type of process which best suits the individual or group concerned, and the particular decision to be made. In essence, there are two types of decision-making process, logical and instinctive (Hopson and Scally 1987c). The logical process is common, and as it has the most easily identifiable steps, it is the easiest to teach directly (Fig 5.3).

FIG 5.3: THE LOGICAL DECISION-MAKING PROCESS

Step 1	What decision is to be made?
Step 2	What is the belief system within which the decision is to be made?
Step 3	What are the options?
Step 4	What information is needed?
Step 5	How can the information become accessible?
Step 6	What are the options in the light of the newly-acquired information?
Step 7	What are the advantages and disadvantages of each option?
Step 8	Which is the best option?

The instinctive process refers to decisions made on the basis of emotions and intuition. As students become more self-confident and more aware of their emotions, they will start to trust themselves and therefore trust and enhance their ability to make instinctive decisions. Since this process does not necessarily involve logical thought and there are no identifiable steps involved, there is a tendency to negate it as a valid method for making decisions. However, it is frequently used, possibly more frequently than some people acknowledge. How many times do we explore the advantages and disadvantages of a number of options, having already made a choice based on emotions and intuition? Usually, a combination of the instinctive and logical approach is most appropriate.

The majority of decisions cannot be seen in terms of "right" and "wrong" but rather as opportunities for development. However, there are some decisions about practical tasks which will lead to success or failure. While students should not always be protected from making mistakes, teacher and student should work together to find the appropriate solution so that the student can be guarded against repeated failure as this can be demoralising. Some decision-making is influenced by safety and risk-taking issues. Legal restraints exist on the amount and type of risk a school can condone. Within these constraints, students and parents should be aware of the risks and then be allowed to decide on a course of action together.

Making choices involves taking responsibility for those choices. Young people with physical disabilities who need personal care assistance of any form, sometimes need to take account of more factors than their able-bodied peers. For example, if a young person living in a residential school may want to go out in the evening and arrive home at 10.30 p.m., when the the night staff are on duty. She may have decided to go, knowing that she will be tired the next day: that should be her choice. However, if she goes, she also has to arrange care staff cover in advance so that she can get to bed in the evening. In order to take responsibility for her choice, she has to learn and use the skills involved in negotiating for assistance at the time she wants it. She is not taking responsibility for her choice if she expects someone will be there when it suits her. Furthermore, she is not being given the opportunity to take responsibility for her choice if the care staff arrange how to provide the necessary cover without consulting her.

It is essential that schools encourage young people to practice the decision-making skills taught, in real situations with real consequences (see for example sections on "providing a broad range of experiences", on page **73** and "self-care" on page **100**). It is equally important that schools emphasise the importance of decision-making skills to parents, so that if parents agree, they too can foster these skills in a similar way. This can be particularly difficult for those caring for and working with young people with severe communication difficulties as there is often a need to guess what they are trying to say (see page **90**). It is important to give young people time to communicate their decisions so that they can choose to act in a way which might not fit others' perception of them. Schools can facilitate the development of decision-making skills by setting up school meetings and self-advocacy groups.

School meetings (councils) encourage students to look at school rules and sanctions, and are forums for discussion and voting on school matters that are brought to the attention of the meeting. In small schools with school councils, each young person and staff member has one vote on school matters and in large schools, representatives are democratically elected and given voting rights within the meeting. Those as young as 11 years old, once taught the processes of decision making, can exercise these skills if they are encouraged to do so. However, given institutional and legal constraints, and philosophical frameworks, it is important that schools give clear messages about what is open for debate and what is not. It is counter-productive to encourage discussion about a school rule if the views of the school meeting would not effect any change in any case.

Advocacy groups usually comprise eight to twelve members who meet voluntarily on a weekly basis to discuss any matters relevant to the members. They run their own meetings, work together to understand common difficulties and find solutions to these problems (Gould and McTaggart 1988). School meetings and self-advocacy groups not only provide opportunities to develop decision-making skills but also provide peer models and peer support in decision making.

MANAGING EMOTIONS AND CONFLICT

The first essential skill for managing emotions is being able to acknowledge that we are experiencing an emotion! Many people are so out of touch with what they feel that they are unable to articulate anything clearly. The question "How are you?" is commonly answered with the socially acceptable "I'm fine thank you" or "O.K." – people rarely answer with how they feel. Although it would be inappropriate to always answer with a detailed statement, it is suggested than many people lack the skills to be able to identify and thus manage their emotions.

In essence, emotions can be divided into two categories – positive emotions and negative emotions. Positive emotions are pleasent feelings and negative emotions are feelings that are more difficult to cope with eg. anger, depression, fear, jealousy, envy and anxiety. Expression of negative emotions, in particular, is generally considered unacceptable within society. In this country, the pervading British "stiff upper lip" mentality promotes the suppression of fear and anger, and the masking of depression. This can leave a person thinking that her feelings are unacceptable, whilst others are saved from the demands of dealing with an individual's negative emotions. This can quickly lead into a vicious circle with an individual unable to accept and express her own negative emotions and unlikely to give opportunities to others to express theirs.

Everyone experiences a variety of emotions, but they will be expressed in different ways by each individual. Paradoxically, many negative emotions are healthy and an important part of all human beings. They cannot be totally eliminated, and any attempt to do so may simply result in their becoming suppressed. This suppression can lead to the emotions becoming intensified, and sometimes expressed in other, apparently unrelated ways. For example, a young person may become acutely depressed because she has been rejected by someone with whom she wanted to have a relationship. These feelings of rejection may reinforce other similar feelings from the past and raise anxiety about the future, so her acute depression may appear to others as an over-reaction.

Schools should encourage young people to begin to clarify some of the reasons why they act and react in the way they do. Most people's expression follows patterns, so if each individual could begin to identify her patterns, she would become more self-empowered and more able to manage emotional situations. In the example above, if she, through explicit sessions on managing emotions, became aware that her feelings result from more than rejection by one person, then she may be able to start to change her reactions, and would have the choice about whether or not she wished to explore the other causes in more intensive counselling.

It can be difficult to cope with conflicting emotions and desires. For example, the desire for independence is unlikely to be simple for any individual. At the same time as desiring independence, young people may also require that certain limitations be set down by adults. Adolescence is generally the period when the conflict between the need for dependence and independence is most intense. It could be argued that for young people who need personal care assistance, the conflict is more complex. Their physical dependency needs may mean that there is considerable anger directed towards their parents on whom they are dependent (Kennett 1986). Those who no longer need physical care assistance may feel lonely and miss the company and the emotional support they had from their personal care assistants. On the one hand they may desire independence, but on the other hand, they may also want to be looked after. This conflict can lead to some young people needing and seeking a lot of attention from adults. If young people are unable to identify and express their conflicts, their emotions may well become all-consuming. They may feel guilty about their negative feelings which they find unpalatable even though these are to be expected and are part of the processes of growing, becoming independent and of coming to terms with their disability.

Young people should be taught the skills of expressing their emotions appropriately, in a constructive manner: skills which are taught on many assertiveness training courses. For example, although anger is as uncomfortable to experience as to receive, it is possible to learn to direct anger appropriately and to use it to effect change rather than be overwhelmed by it. This may entail taking time away from the situation and learning how to communicate angry feelings to others without fear of losing the relationship with them and in a way which enables all those involved to move forward.

Many able-bodied young people initially express anger and conflicting feelings by running away, engaging in physically aggressive play or just taking time out to be away from people. Some young people with mobility difficulties may not have access to these opportunities and alternative forms of expression should be sought. Pushing young people to express verbally anger and conflicts, such as the one posed above, can simply reinforce their anxieties. Other expressive media, such as art or drama may allow conflicts to be discussed through the use of symbols, so enabling students to distance themselves from their problems and thereby making the exploration process safer (Kennett 1986). In fact, for young people with communication difficulties, these media can be particularly helpful.

In essence, the basic skills of managing emotions are acknowledging and identifying emotions we are experiencing, expressing our emotions appropriately, understanding why we feel the way we do, and changing our patterns of behaviour to manage our emotions more effectively. This is easier said than done, but it is possible to facilitate the development of these skills through explicit group discussion/activity sessions which ideally, should be run by two professionals trained in group work skills (see page **148**). Two facilitators are needed so that one can basically lead the session and the other can be more sensitive to individual reactions at any given time. If the facilitators cannot be fully trained, there is a danger that the group will be counter-productive and frightening for all group members. Those wanting to run sessions on managing emotions should have some basic training, supervision by someone qualified in group work, and adequate support from other staff. Some young people may need more support than can be offered through these sessions, so individual counselling with a qualified counsellor, may be additionally appropriate.

MANAGING GRIEF AND LOSS

In essence, Kubler-Ross (1969) defined the stages involved in grieving as shock, denial, bargaining, anger, depression and acceptance. Together, these serve as guidelines for the grieving process, which can best be understood within the context of the family, taking into account the cultural and religious frameworks, the support available and the individual's past history. Although each individual expresses and comes to terms with her feelings in different ways, problems may arise when emotions are denied for long periods of time, and the grief is left to fester unacknowledged. Whilst it is unwise to push individuals into expressing emotions when they are not ready to do so, it is important that young people have the space to express and explore emotions when they do wish to do so. It is equally important that parents and professionals attempt to clarify their roles in enabling young people to learn about loss and death.

All major life events involve change and thus some form of loss. There are many different kinds of loss which can cause grief. Separation from a friend, parent or sibling through death or otherwise, can lead to a period of mourning for the individual concerned. It has been argued that young people with acquired impairments need to grieve for the loss of the affected part of their body (Speck 1978). More contentiously, some believe that the acceptance of congenital disability also involves a mourning period. Each loss can be seen as a "little death" and how each is dealt with will affect how each individual deals with her own death and others close to her.

The reasons why some adults feel the need to protect children from death probably arises from their own fears and attitudes, rather than those of the children. It is more likely that children try to protect adults from the pain, by responding to adults' fear and the societal message that death is not spoken about (Dominica 1987). Research evidence suggests that adult concepts of loss and death are present in those aged as young as 11 (Liddell 1982; Wolff 1974).

Given that this is the case and accepting the concept of loss outlined, there is a need to make education about loss and death an integral part of learning for living for all students. However, the need is most urgent for young people with progressive conditions who have to face the concept of death earlier than most. The dearth of literature on working with young people with progressive conditions suggests this is an area that many people find very painful.

On visiting both ordinary and special schools, the researcher was told either that students with progressive conditions were treated the same as other students or they were excluded from lessons deemed inappropriate eg. Lessons for Living. Many staff felt unprepared to meet the specific emotional needs of young people with progressive conditions, saying that they relied purely on instinct. However, for many adults, instinct may involve denying young people's conditions and avoiding awkward questions. If professionals are to help young people come to terms with the rest of their lives, it is important that they can accept the young people's conditions and endeavour to face their own death with equanimity. Research has shown that the need for denial in patients with serious illnesses is directly related to their doctor's need for denial (Kubler-Ross 1969b). In other words, doctors who can talk to their patients about their conditions will find their patients more accepting, and those who themselves need denial will find it in their patients. It is likely that this process is the same for nurses and other professionals in schools, who work with young people with deteriorating conditions. Therefore, schools should ensure that staff have the time and space to address their own fears and attitudes towards death and progressive conditions.

Anger can be one of the most difficult parts of the grieving process, and so a clear strategy is needed for staff to deal with it effectively. Young people with progressive conditions and their families may direct their anger at staff within schools who are offering them support. This sets up a difficult situation as these young people and their families may unwittingly ostracise themselves at a time when they are most in need of support. It is important for staff to try to recognise the anger and to stand by them however they behave so that they can work through the anger and panic that they need to show (Walters 1982).

Literature has suggested that young people with progressive conditions usually appreciate frank information about their conditions and open discussions about death (Liddell 1982). Generally, parents are expected to provide this information, and discuss death with their child. However, research conducted with boys with Duchenne Muscular Dystrophy and their families, suggests that parents often find this very difficult, and avoid their child's poignant comments to avoid the anxiety which accompanies their mutual feelings (Witte 1985). Although some parents were ambivalent about their lack of direct communication within the family, others felt guilty about ignoring their sons' worries, but none actively wanted to withhold information from their sons. Many parents need as much help in coming to terms with progressive illness and death as their child. Without this, they cannot always communicate with their child even though improved communication would be likely to help the whole family. In any case, young people often do know about their conditions whether or not they have been explicitly told, although they may have some distorted information passed down by peers. Wolff (1974) found that after telling children about their condition, they stated that they had already known and were relieved that they no longer had to keep it secret. They were also able to take support to mourn what was and might have been in relation to their deteriorating bodies. The following poem is one teenager's expression of her impending death.

WATER

I noticed it on Monday,
A tiny patch of damp,
On the ceiling,
In the corner,
Above the standard lamp.

On Tuesday, was it growing?
Could anyone be sure?
But,
By Wednesday morning,
It was dripping on the floor.

Thursday, I phoned for the plumber,
He said "Oh it'll stop",
Friday,
When it hadn't,
He brought me round a mop.

The weekend was a nightmare,
Of dry house I would dream,
But lo,
On Monday morning,
My puddle became a stream.

The situation worsened,
There was nothing I could do,
In fact,
To reach the kitchen,
I had to paddle a canoe.

In the end my house departed,
I think it joined the sea,
And I?
I ended up in hospital,
With water on the knee.

R J Goldsmith *Aged 14*

Rebecca Goldsmith died in June 1986.

It is suggested that medical staff within schools should give young people the option to discuss their conditions with them, unless parents explicitly forbid it, so that they can allay any unfounded fears and can help young people come to terms with the rest of their lives and their remaining fears.

It could be argued that talking about emotions surrounding loss and death in general, is better left as a taboo rather than dealt with openly but inappropriately. As stated before, it is certainly true that amateur counselling can be counter-productive and even dangerous for all concerned. However, staff should be adequately supported and trained to conduct explicit group sessions and to know that they can feel confident about referring to a qualified counsellor any individual who appears to need to explore her feelings more extensively.

DEVELOPING SEXUALITY

"Sexuality, . . . is not something which we happen to have but a basic and integral part of what we are. People everywhere are sexual beings and without sexuality we should be less human. Sex and sexuality are built into the structure of our mental and physical processes and we can never escape them." Stewart (1979).

We can deny, repress or use our sexuality effectively but it is a part of us commencing at birth and ending at death. Sexual practice is, to some extent, socially defined and, as such, is influenced by peers, religion, economics, the media, law and the family. Within sex education both practical and ethical issues need to be explored. This requires that professionals and parents are aware of their own views and prejudices.

There are many ways in which people, both able-bodied and disabled, can choose to express their sexuality including heterosexuality, celibacy, bisexuality and homosexuality. We cannot assume that all disabled people are heterosexual and to do so is heterosexist. Heterosexism can be defined as a system of values and practices based on a set of beliefs about heterosexuality being the only normal and natural sexuality for both women and men. Heterosexism lays down the rules and conditions under which all sexualities are valued and devalued: penalties and benefits are accordingly awarded under heterosexism – lesbians and gay men are particularly penalised. Some disabled people may well be lesbian or gay and as such, are doubly oppressed, as society is somewhat intolerant of people who are not considered "normal"! If a young person is or chooses to be lesbian or gay, there is a danger that this will be seen as a problem stemming from an inability to adjust to disability. This is reflected in research which, on finding some young people with disabilities to be uninterested in people of the opposite sex, suggested this was due to embarrassment about their impairments (eg. Dorner 1977). Although this may be true for some, it assumes that all those in the study were, or wished to be, heterosexual.

But there is research to suggest that on average 10% of the general population are predominantly lesbian or gay (Kinsey *et al.* 1984; Kinsey *et al.* 1953; Weinberg and Williams 1974). Furthermore, no source estimates that less than 5% of the entire population is lesbian or gay (Babuscio 1988). There is no reason to suppose that the distribution in terms of sexual orientation is any different in the population of people with disabilities. However, it must be recognised that many persons' sexual orientation is neither absolute nor a constant. Whilst some people may define themselves as exclusively lesbian, gay or heterosexual, others have both heterosexual and lesbian or gay experiences. Thus, it is argued that sexual orientation should be seen as a continuum with very few people at either extreme, and that all sex education should take account of the needs of all people who are at different points on the spectrum.

| Exclusively heterosexual | ——————————————— | Exclusively lesbian/gay |

There are many myths surrounding sexuality and disability (McKown 1986) which some young people with disabilities may absorb so that they themselves believe them. First, people with disabilities are seen as sexless. Although schools do not perpetuate this explicitly, some personal care practice does little to counteract this general myth (see page **109**). A contrasting myth claims that people with disabilities, particularly those with learning difficulties, have uncontrollable sexual urges. It is true that some young people with disabilities may display "inappropriate" sexual behaviour, eg. openly masturbating in public, displaying affection to strangers, forcing sexual contact on others without their consent, or taking clothes off in public. However "inappropriate", sexual behaviour is inevitably socially and culturally defined and people with learning difficulties are more frequently thought to display "inappropriate" behaviour than the rest of the population. This is often because of the attitudes of those labelling the young people and/or the lack of other outlets for young people with learning difficulties to express their sexuality. Whilst most staff and parents do not condone "inappropriate" sexual behaviour, they may be inadvertently encouraging it by infantalising young people with disabilities, or by passing on some of the myths outlined in this section. It is important to look at "inappropriate" sexual behaviour in relation to society's attitudes to sexuality and disability. The attitudes of significant people (eg. parents and carers) are also important as are the physical environment, social life, and the quality of sex education received.

Lack of privacy is a major problem for young people with mobility difficulties as many do not have access to secret places like able-bodied young people do. It is generally recognised that many young people learn from their "behind the bike shed" experiences, but some miss this informal education because they are unable to get there. Ideally, the "bike sheds" should be made more physically accessible, but if this is not feasible, schools may need to contrive an area where disabled young people can have privacy.

Social isolation, and the lack of peer contact outside school hours is clearly a limiting factor for young people learning the skills of forming and maintaining relationships that are defined by them as sexual in nature. This lack of opportunity is one of the essential limiting factors to developing and maintaining sexual relationships in adulthood (Leahy 1982). Lack of access to informal sex education from peers is a barrier for some young people with disabilities. Dorner (1977) found that parents and schools were the main sources of heterosexual sex education for the interviewees with disabilities at all schools in his study, while the able-bodied interviewees derived most of their information from peers. However, those with disabilities educated in ordinary schools were more likely to have learned about heterosexual sex from their peers than those in special schools. Other research has shown that many parents find it difficult to communicate with their children about sex and personal relationships and many do not see themselves as "good sex educators" (Allen 1987). It is likely that many lesbian and gay young people with disabilities will receive misinformation from peers, and possibly from parents, about their sexuality. Thus for all young people, sex education in school is very important, but for those with disabilities in special schools, and for all those exploring being lesbian or gay, it needs to be particularly thorough given the difficulties outlined above.

Other myths relate to sexual functioning: the belief that people with disabilities cannot experience sexual pleasure assumes that sexual pleasure is confined to a specific act or organ. It also ignores the fact that sexual pleasure can be derived from giving as well as receiving. Where recognised, sexual problems of and issues relating to people with disabilities are assumed to be automatically related to their impairments, even though the range of problems highlighted by people with disabilities reflects those commonly found in the whole population. For example, research has suggested that, in particular, boys with disabilities tend to worry about their capacity for sexual intercourse and their ability to derive pleasure from it (Dorner 1977; Anderson and Clarke 1982c). Many young people with disabilities believe their impairments make them unattractive to others. Young people with lower limb paralysis often perceive sexual functions to be the same as sexual identity, therefore they are likely to see themselves more negatively. Besides, although some people with disabilities may experience less sensation, alternative areas which elicit sexual feelings can be identified. Some young people with disabilities need information seeking skills and access to information about how their impairments affect their sexual functioning, if at all (see page **79**).

There are also myths about with whom it is appropriate for people with disabilities to have sexual relationships. It is often assumed that people with disabilities should only have sexual relationships with others with disabilities. This attitude makes the disability the definer of a person. It suggests that people with disabilities are less worthy and unable to develop sexual relationships on the same premise as able-bodied people. This is reflected in another myth which suggests that an able-bodied person who chooses to marry or live with someone disabled must have problems of her own! Furthermore, for many young people with disabilities it is seen as a status symbol to have an able-bodied heterosexual partner, probably indicating how they see themselves. Sometimes, an able-bodied person may "go out" with a disabled person out of pity rather than genuine desire, so once again, making the disability the main definer of a person. For example, it can be the case that a disabled young person at a youth club "goes out" with the able-bodied young people once, but rarely more than that whereas if the disabled individual was able-bodied, she would have been unlikely to "go out" with anyone. It is important to encourage able-bodied young people to recognise their fear of offending others and to be aware of their pity and to realise that honest, sensitive communication is less hurtful in the long term.

The final myth to be considered here is that women with disabilities will automatically have children with a disability. However, whilst few disabilities are thought to be genetically determined, research is always changing with new technological advances. It is important to recognise that a congenital impairment is not the same as an hereditary impairment. A congenital impairment is not necessarily hereditary and an hereditary impairment is not always present at birth. Even where genetic factors are implicated, this does not mean that all offspring would be affected. Many young people have needless worries about genetic risks; girls about their ability to conceive and the likelihood of having a child with a similar impairment and boys, about their potency (Dorner, 1976; Anderson and Clarke 1982d). Genetic counselling should be readily available to young people with disabilities and their families, requiring expert knowledge on the risks of transmitting various impairments and the possible health risks of childbirth. Genetic counselling is defined as "a communication process about the problems related to the existence of, or chances of, a hereditary disability in a family" (American Society of Human Studies). Genetic counsellors have special medical training and are the most qualified to pass on genetic information. However, it seems rare that they see young people under the age of 16 without full family histories and full parental involvement to which young people often object. For this reason, and also because of poor communication between medical and educational services, information about genetic factors remains inaccessible to many young people with disabilities.

Gaining better access to genetic information also involves the need to address the question of abortion. Genetic implications are often presented in the form that all rational people would want their pregnancy terminated if an abnormality is detected. This assumes that having children with disabilities is automatically traumatic. In fact, since people with disabilities generally have more experience of disability than the general population, they may be more equipped to handle any problems which may arise. It is important that the question of abortion is handled very sensitively with young people with disabilities, as it will inevitably raise questions as to the person's own right to life.

All schools visited in the present study provided some form of sex education. The plans for general sex education outlined in the ordinary schools visited appeared clearer and better documented than those in the majority of special schools. However, participation in sex education in ordinary schools may not be sufficient as students with disabilities may feel that some of the lessons are irrelevant to them. Most sex education focuses on anatomy, physiology and sexually transmitted diseases within an able-bodied heterosexist framework. There is a tendency within all types of provision to avoid ethics and values, concepts of love, maturity and sexuality. This may be because of a lack of definition of these terms (Haight and Fachting 1986). But these issues must be addressed if young people are to develop and maintain fulfilling sexual relationships in their adult lives.

Issues specifically related to disability and/or particular impairments should be addressed in all schools, for instance feelings about asking out an able-bodied peer as well as the more physical concerns discussed earlier in this section. In ordinary schools, it may be more appropriate to offer individualised support and/or a segregated course in addition to regular sex education lessons, rather than to incorporate these issues into the regular curriculum, given the stigma attached to sexuality and disability (see page **136**).

In the special schools visited, a structured sex education curriculum for young people with learning difficulties was being devised. These students were thought to find it hard to retain basic information like the names of body parts, so it is important to be sensitive to the slang they generally use. Staff were acutely aware of the fine line between giving young people with learning difficulties too much information and too little. Students, parents and professionals should work together to find the appropriate balance. It is essential that if parents wish, they can be actively involved in the sex education of their child. It may be helpful to run groups for parents where, initially, they could discuss their own attitudes to sexuality and disability and clarify the messages they want to convey. The group could also decide to look at effective ways of communicating with their children and to gain access to information about the implications of their child's impairments on sexual functioning.

Since parents often identify the school nurse as the key professional concerned with the sexuality of young people with disabilities (Tse and Opie 1986), it could be argued that the school nurse should be involved with any support to parents offered through group work. However, so as to not reinforce the association between medical care and sexuality, at least one non-medical member of the multi-disciplinary teams needs to facilitate the group. To reiterate, it is important that any staff members facilitating a group such as this, are aware of their own attitudes and have the necessary groupwork skills, eg. staff such as occupational therapists, social workers, and counsellors.

There is a need for more staff training and more published material which address the many aspects of sexuality and disability, particularly for young people with learning difficulties. The question of sexuality is contentious and fraught with many difficulties which many find easier to ignore. However, it is an essential part of becoming more self-empowered and if ignored, young people are effectively being denied their basic human rights.

CHAPTER SIX
Learning

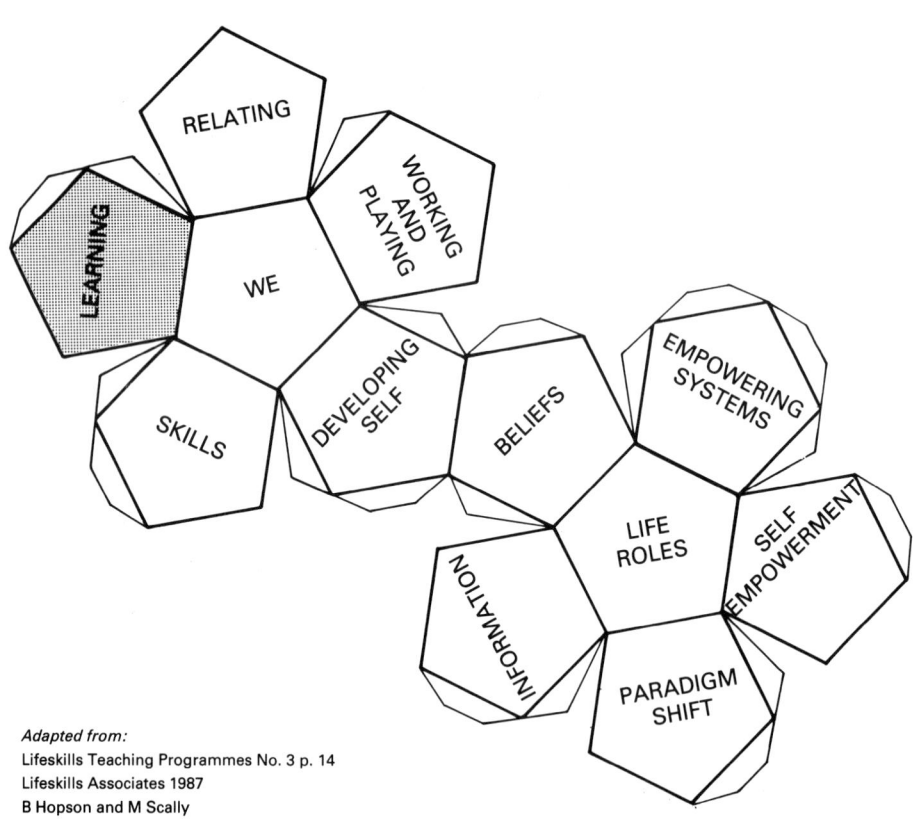

Adapted from:
Lifeskills Teaching Programmes No. 3 p. 14
Lifeskills Associates 1987
B Hopson and M Scally

Learning is defined as the acquisition of knowledge or skills through direct or vicarious experience, which may result in a change of behaviour.

This chapter focuses on knowledge and skills which are helpful to young people with disabilities, although much of it is equally relevant to parents and staff alike. In the first part of the chapter, some suggestions are made of ways to broaden the experiences of young people with disabilities, and some skills of learning from experience are discussed. In the second part, information-seeking skills are discussed in relation to information about the self, others and the system.

PROVIDING A BROAD RANGE OF EXPERIENCES

As can be seen from the comments given in Table 3.1, young people with disabilities are frequently over-protected and have limited life experiences compared with their able-bodied peers. An empowering education system should seek to redress this balance by offering students a very wide range of experiences from which to learn.

Within school:

Whilst it is desirable to work towards independence in specific therapy sessions and living skills lessons, it is widely recognised that "independence" is not just one lesson at a specified time on the timetable. This section offers a few suggestions of how aspects of the school day can be used to promote independence.

There is a danger that some young people with disabilities are socialised into being passive recipients of other people's help. They often lack the opportunities to take on a measure of responsibility for others within their lives, and this makes it more difficult for them to learn how to be active members of a community. It may be helpful if students with disabilities are given specific responsibilities within a particular lesson, or within their year group. Responsibility for even small tasks, such as watering classroom plants, can provide a simple, effective way to improve individual young people's sense of control and self-confidence.

Using cafeteria services is another good way of promoting independence within the school. It enables young people to choose what and when to eat within the lunch break. They learn both to negotiate a queue and to budget to afford the items they enjoy. If an individual is unable to serve or/and eat without help, she could learn to arrange for care staff cover at a time which is mutually convenient for her and the member of care staff concerned.

Although all ordinary and some special schools visited during this study operate some kind of canteen system, the majority of special schools serve students at set tables and many of the above learning opportunities are missed. Some of these special schools place staff on each table even when they are not needed as enablers. Although this "family service" system can offer opportunities for the development of conversational skills, helpfulness and appropriate table manners, these opportunities exist less artificially within the cafeteria system. Furthermore, cafeteria systems offer more implicit empowering messages to the young people using them than "family service" systems.

Integration and Segregation

Students with disabilities being educated in special schools need to have opportunities to socialise with their able-bodied peers. This widely accepted notion is reflected in link schemes operating between all the special schools visited and their local ordinary schools. These schemes have been found to be of benefit to all those involved (Jowett *et al.* 1988). For some young people with disabilities, it may be necessary to create "artificial" opportunities, at first through clubs such as PHAB (Physically Handicapped and Able-Bodied), so that natural friendships can begin to develop.

It is equally important that students within ordinary schools are given the opportunity to develop two peer groups – age peers and disabled peers with whom they have experiences in common (Gould 1986). Whilst integration is a commendable aim, it can be difficult and isolating for a young person with a disability to integrate herself fully into an ordinary school, particularly if there are only one or two other students with disabilities within the school. In order to cope, she may over-compensate by working excessively hard at academic work, or she may try to pretend that she does not have a disability, so stopping herself from learning the specific mechanistic skills needed to live more independently (Heumann *et al.* 1987). There may be times when she would appreciate the support and empathy which she can only get from a disabled peer, as she may feel that her able-bodied friends' experiences are culturally different from her own. Schools could meet this need by setting up voluntary school/borough support groups and/or peer counselling sessions where disabled young people could set their own agenda (see page **23**).

Community Facilities

Programmes working explicitly towards independence must, wherever possible, be conducted in the "real" environment rather than in artificial situations, as this enhances students' motivation and maximises on a variety of teaching opportunities. For example, even when a student is at the most basic stage of counting, she can practice these skills by shopping in the community. Counting by twos can also be practised by noting the street numbers on buildings when looking for a given address (Gow and Horban 1986). Other skills, eg. road safety and using public transport, are also easier to learn if taught in the real environment, as students can perceive the advantages that success brings.

It is also helpful if schools use other community facilities as much as possible, eg. local swimming baths, community centres and libraries. This provides opportunities for students to learn how to use these local facilities and how to gather information from them (see page **81**). Students could participate in arrangements for some of these visits so they can develop organisational skills, eg. arranging transport, checking access and parking facilities.

Within residential settings, young people should be encouraged to arrange their social life, including negotiating necessary care staff cover for themselves if they want to arrive home late. Even younger children can play some active part in this process with the enabling support of staff. Although organised outings have their place, they should not be the sole recreational/ social format because they tend to diminish opportunities for many learning experiences. Wherever possible students should be encouraged to participate in the arrangements for such organised outings.

Extra-School Activities

A broad range of experiences can be provided through an innovative programme of extra-school activities. Active participation in, for example, school plays, fetes, sports, and community service can help students become more self-confident and enhance their motivation in learning the essentially boring skills of maintenance time (see page **97**). Many of the schools visited mentioned that lack of adequate transport provided by LEAs meant that many students with disabilities could not stay for activities after school. Thus it would seem that the young people who most need structured activities of this kind to widen their range of experiences, are often unable to attend. Whilst we argue that LEAs should provide this transport after statutory school hours, disabled students, their parents and the school could also work together to find alternative means of transport for occasional events, so that these valuable activities are not missed.

The majority of special schools and some ordinary schools visited during this study use the Duke of Edinburgh Award Scheme to encourage young people with disabilities to broaden their experiences. This scheme, open to those aged fourteen years and above, is divided into four sections: service, expeditions, skills and physical recreation (Duke of Edinburgh Award Handbook 1988). All these sections have many options which are open to young people with disabilities. There is a similar adapted scheme for young people with learning difficulties organised by Gateway Clubs. School holidays are also valuable as young people with disabilities tend to have less opportunities to spend time away from their home environment, especially if they are physically dependent on adults. In particular, Outward Bound courses help young people assume more control over their environment and develop a more positive body image. Parents of participants have described their children as more outgoing, assertive and self-confident after a course (Kessell *et al*. 1985). These courses should be given greater prominence in the priorities of schools and local education authorities.

Learning from Experience

> "This whole train of experiencing, and the meanings that I have thus far discovered in it, seem to have launched me on a process which is both fascinating and at times a little frightening. It seems to mean letting my experience carry me on, in a direction which appears to me forward, towards goals that I can dimly define, as I try to understand at least the current meaning of that experience. The sensation is that of floating with a complex stream of experience, with the fascinating possibility of trying to comprehend its ever changing complexity". Carl Rogers (1967)

The skills of reflecting, assessing and evaluating personal experiences can enable young people to develop greater insight into these experiences and subsequently to learn from them. By starting to identify their thoughts, feelings and behaviours, they can take more and more responsibility for their learning.

Passivity, lack of motivation and poor self-image have been highlighted as factors which inhibit the development of independence (see Table 3.1). These factors are consistent with the theory of learned helplessness and reflect society's attitudes to people with disabilities, and underlie the process of structural iatrogenesis (page **22**). These are limiting attitudes and behaviours which are more likely to have been learnt at an early age, becoming more entrenched over time. They will colour attitudes towards, and perceptions of the future which will affect a person's present learning (Rosenthal and Jacobson 1968). For example, the girl who believes she will not get a job and will never leave home, is more likely to make those beliefs a reality than the girl who believes she has more control over her life. This is not intended to invalidate the economic reality, but to put it in some perspective.

Young people with disabilities should be encouraged to see the learning potential in all their past and present experiences. Making mistakes and taking risks are both rich sources of learning (Heumann 1987). Young people should not be allowed to struggle to the point of exhaustion, but they should not be protected from making mistakes. With the many pressures on the school day, it is often difficult to allow opportunity for learning in this way because it is time-consuming to watch individuals struggle and then to talk through with them what they have learnt and how they could make the task easier in the future.

Students should be taught to ask themselves questions about their behaviours, thoughts and feelings before, during and after as many difficult experiences as possible, ie. to develop individualised "self-review" questions (Pearce *et al*. 1982). They should also be encouraged to analyse the external factors which helped them to be successful in any given task and how these factors could be improved. Young people with the skills to reflect and build upon their experiences in this way are more likely to be able to generalise learning from one situation to another (Pearce *et al*. 1982).

Some disabilities have particular problems associated with them. For example, some young people with hydrocephalus experience problems with transferring skills. Sequencing, spatial and perceptual difficulties, and short-term memory deficits are the main reasons for this. Although these are thought to be mainly physiological impairments, there are ways to facilitate more effective learning: since many young people with hydrocephalus and other learning difficulties find it difficult to perform elements of a task in the correct order, they have to be taught specifically how to sequence these elements. As for everyone, concise simple instructions should be repeated, given possible problems with short-term memory (Holgate 1985). They should also be allowed time generally to orientate themselves to a new environment and to relearn the specific skills they need. For instance, a young person with hydrocephalus who has learned a bathing routine at school, should be given help to transfer the skills to the home because everything is differently arranged there. Young people with hydrocephalus and other learning difficulties might also benefit from the use of the self-reflective skills outlined earlier in this section.

INFORMATION-SEEKING SKILLS

There is a wealth of information within modern society which can enable adults with disabilities to become more self-empowered. Much of this information, however, may not take into account the needs of young people from minority ethnic groups (Perkin and Nathwani 1987). Unless adults with disabilities have the confidence and skills to work through complex bureaucracies and/or to question potentially intimidating experts, this information can remain inaccessible to them. For this reason, many voluntary agencies have set up information services which try to decode some of the information into everyday language and help to put individuals in contact with the appropriate people to help them with their query (see Appendix 2).

When young people with disabilities are at school, they are often in regular contact with professionals (eg. occupational therapists and careers officers) who have some of this self-empowering information. Thus, the school years appear to be an ideal time to provide students with as much information as possible, since many of these services are less accessible to them when they leave school (Thomas *et al.* 1987). This is the theory behind the information-centred approach to teaching living skills. However, it is unlikely that young people with disabilities will retain information which they do not need nor see the value of, at the time they are being taught it. Furthermore, there is a vast quantity of information available and eligibility criteria and benefits frequently change. Therefore, it is not only impossible to teach it all, but also impossible to anticipate the information an individual may need in the future. Thus, teaching ways to gain access to information and how to use it, is more valuable in the long-term than a purely information-centred approach, although the two approaches overlap. Students should be encouraged to identify and request the information they want, so that they can start to take more responsibility for their own learning. The implementation of the whole holographic model should do this. More specifically, participation in developing and assessing their own living skills programmes will help to identify gaps in their knowledge and develop self-confidence, and the skills of assertiveness will enable them to to ask more questions.

Students with disabilities should also be taught ways to gain access to information outside the school environment and the skills of using it to their best advantage. It is unwise to make generalisations, but it is possible to identify certain key skills and areas of knowledge that may be helpful.

1. The skills of identifying what one does not know but which would be useful.
2. A knowledge of services and individuals who may help gain access to the needed information.
3. The skills of specifying the exact information required and communicating this to the appropriate people, eg. assertiveness skills.
4. The skills to contact the individual or service, eg. using telephones, writing/typing letters, using libraries, community services.
5. The skills of monitoring the progress from the contacts made.

The next section offers some suggestions on ways to help young people develop information-seeking skills. The section is subdivided into information about the self, others and the "system". From the results of this study and recommendations from other research reports, it highlights some useful information for young people with disabilities. There may be times when it is inappropriate to give information when students have not developed the skills and understanding to be able to use it wisely. You will be able to help students choose the specific amount of information which is most relevant for them at any particular time.

INFORMATION

Information about the Self

Young people with disabilities will become more aware of their abilities, strengths, limitations and potential by developing the skills of learning from experience (outlined earlier in this chapter) and the skills of giving and receiving feedback to and from peers (see page **91**). Participation in extra-school activities and an enabling leisure skills component to a living skills curriculum will help students identify their interests (see page **125**). Finally, active participation in their assessments, including valued self-assessments can also enable students to learn more about themselves (see page **141**). A positive self-image can both enhance and be enhanced by this knowledge and by skill development (Chapter Five).

It is equally important that students with disabilities develop an understanding of their individual impairment and resulting disabilities (Dorner 1976) to become more self-empowered.* The present study shows that approximately 40% of student interviewees did not know the medical description of their impairments, allowing for instances where their condition had not been specified by the medical profession. For example, 42% students with Cerebral Palsy were unable to recall this information when interviewed.

The majority of young people with disabilities acquire information about their disability from their parents (Anderson and Clarke 1982d). However, the results of this study show that 11% of parents were also unable to give this information when interviewed. It is not possible to conclude from this data that these interviewees have never been given this information, but it is reasonable to say they had not absorbed it, possibly because it was painful or disturbing, or because they were confused at the time the information was imparted.

It is essential that schools have structured procedures to ensure that young disabled people know the medical description and develop a good understanding of their disability. Professionals need to repeat the information in a variety of different ways at regular intervals, and to check out that it has been absorbed. Group lessons for students with similar impairments should cover general, basic facts complemented by individual sessions where young people have the opportunity to raise issues which they may find embarrassing within a group format (see page **136**). Young people need to air their fears openly and need questions answered honestly, sensitively and clearly. If the individual staff member does not know the information requested, she should either refer the student to someone else or work with the student to find a satisfactory answer to the question.

---

*The issues relating to young people with progressive conditions are discussed in Chapter Five.

Information about Others

Students will become more empowered if they are aware of the roles, abilities, beliefs and limitations of those who work with them. An understanding of the roles of various people in the school can help students understand the purpose of the many professional services available to people with disabilities, thus enabling them to identify who to seek out for different problems when they leave school. Roles of staff within schools overlap and young people will choose to talk to the individual with whom they feel most comfortable. If staff are able to be more explicit about their individual abilities, this knowledge will inform young people's choice. By learning to value each individual's different abilities, they are more likely to start valuing their own.

To reiterate, it is helpful for professionals to explore the belief systems from which they live and work (see page **19**). If staff are able to state some of these beliefs within living skills lessons/sessions, it will help students to see the beliefs as personal beliefs rather than as absolutes. Thus, the student may be more likely to explore her own beliefs, so becoming more self-empowered.

Finally, it would be desirable and empowering for all concerned if staff could learn to state to colleagues and students if they find a particular problem or situation difficult. This is easier said than done. Students would learn that everyone has their limitations and that student needs cannot always be met immediately. On visiting schools, the researcher heard some comments from staff to students, which seemed more to reflect the needs and limitations of staff than the needs of the students concerned. These comments all related to the societal taboos of sex and death, such as "sex is quite boring really", and a comment made to a boy with Duchenne Muscular Dystrophy: "We are all going to die someday". The nervous energy surrounding these comments was probably picked up by the students, and the taboos would thus be perpetuated. The students may also have been unsure if they were to blame for this agitation, and so may be less likely to raise the issues with someone else. However, if the staff members had felt strongly enough, they could have stated that they found it hard to talk about sexuality/death and referred the students to someone else. The students would thus have learnt that even those in authority have their vulnerabilities and would have been more likely to respect the staff member's honesty.

Information about the System

Rights

Devaluing attitudes towards people with disabilities are an acute form of oppression (see Chapter One). Disabled students should be informed of disability rights organisations and their work (eg. British Council of Organisations of People with Disabilities, RADAR and local organisations), and the allied self-advocacy movement (eg. People First), so gaining strength and understanding from adults with disabilities who are trying to change these attitudes. If young people are encouraged to become more aware of the ways in which society depowers people with disabilities, they can put their personal experiences into a wider political context. Through group work and counselling, students with disabilities can begin to examine the devaluing attitudes they may have absorbed. This heightened awareness will enable them to begin to change their own attitudes if they so wish, thereby gaining more control over their lives, ie. becoming more self-empowered.

This section in particular, raises a major conflict between education as an "opening out" process and education as a process to maintain the *status quo*. Since people with disabilities are often treated as second class citizens within the *status quo*, education towards independence must be an "opening out" process. If young people with disabilities are to become more self-empowered and thus take their rightful place within society, the education system has to give students the opportunity to explore these issues.

Adults with disabilities need to have basic information concerning allowances and benefits and the eligibility criteria for them even though this area is extremely complex. Thus, researchers have argued that the topic should be covered within the school curriculum for students aged fourteen and above (Hurst 1985; Mittler and Buckingham 1987). Forty per cent of special schools and 10% of integrated schools visited during this study, said that they covered benefits as part of their school leavers curriculum. However, in many cases this meant one talk per year for those over 16 years. Some schools covered this work in more depth by enlisting the help of a social worker, or specialist health visitors. Inner-city schools in particular have found that parental co-operation is essential if students are to have the opportunity to use their benefits for their intended purpose: if parents are on low incomes, their children's benefits can be used to meet basic family needs, eg., heating and food. Therefore, some of these schools offer sessions to parents as well as students. Some schools have found it most effective to work with parents and students together. Some schools have found that group sessions are confusing for both parents and students because of the range of individual entitlements, therefore they offer individual advice.

Teaching about allowances and benefits requires specialised, up-to-date knowledge, given the complexity of the subject and the ever-changing eligibility criteria. Therefore, it is more important for schools to ensure that students and parents know where to get access to this information (eg. disability organisations, citizen advice bureaux, social workers), rather than endeavour to provide specific advice.

Community Resources

Some schools encourage students to develop throughout their school career a personal file of services and options, which they can use whilst at school and afterwards. These files include information on medical and paramedical services, legal services, career services and disability organisations among many others. Compiling such information involves developing knowledge of the options available to them after school with respect to leisure (both specialist and integrated provision), employment and housing (including the availability and use of paid and voluntary personal care assistance if needed). In this way, they develop information-seeking skills by requesting information of interest to them from the relevant organisations.

Disability Equipment and Adaptations

Equipment and adaptations on the market cover a spectrum of activities of daily living. These include electronic aids, communicators and microcomputers, clothing and dressing aids, domestic aids, incontinence aids and mobility aids. Young people with disabilities need to know what equipment is on the market and exactly how to obtain and use it. They also need access to advice (eg. from occupational therapists) as to the most suitable choice. They should learn where supplies come from and what is and is not available through statutory services and how to access alternative sources of funding. This information is available from NAIDEX, The Disabled Living Foundation and local Aids for Living Centres and disability organisations (see Appendix 2 for details).

CHAPTER SEVEN
Relating

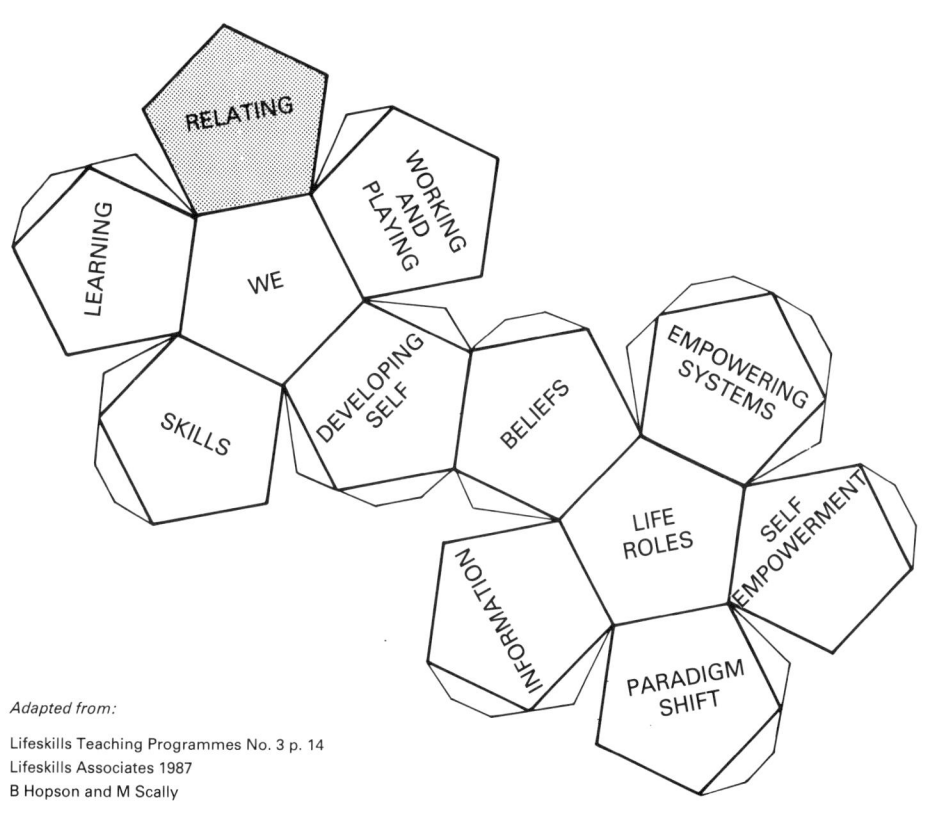

Adapted from:

Lifeskills Teaching Programmes No. 3 p. 14
Lifeskills Associates 1987
B Hopson and M Scally

This chapter begins with the assumption that there is a range of beliefs, attitudes and skills which can enhance the development and maintenance of fulfilling relationships. Essentially, young people are involved in relationships with peers, within the family and with service providers, and it is important to enhance the effectiveness of these relationships. This chapter endeavours to identify and examine facets of relationships which can be addressed within the school curriculum.

RELATIONSHIPS WITH PEERS

The majority of young people do not automatically learn to develop and maintain relationships with peers and act appropriately in social situations (Spence and Shepherd 1983). Young people with disabilities have been found to experience more severe difficulties in social situations than their able-bodied peers (Thomas 1988) and it has been suggested that lack of social skills, poor self-image and frequent social isolation are the major causes of these difficulties (eg. Foster *et al.* 1977). This is supported by the present study which found a trend towards social isolation among the participants. Approximately one-third of the young people interviewed said that they never saw their peers outside school hours (Table 7.1), and the same proportion desired more contact with their peers (Table 7.2).

TABLE 7.1: THE FREQUENCY OF CONTACT WITH PEERS OUTSIDE SCHOOL HOURS

Number of Times Peers Seen	Percentage of Interviewees
Not at all	30
Once a Week	10
2–3 Times a Week	21
4–6 Times a Week	5
Daily	22
Occasionally	12

TABLE 7.2: THE DESIRED CONTACT WITH PEERS OUTSIDE SCHOOL HOURS

Desired Contact with Peers	Percentage of Interviewees
More Often	31
Less Often	3
Same	67

Social isolation not only limits the opportunities open to young people with disabilities to learn and practice their social skills, but is also likely to have a negative effect on their self-image and attitudes towards others. Enabling young people to broaden their range of experiences (see page **73**) and to become aware of and learn to use different methods of transport (see page **119**) will contribute to lessening the problem of social isolation. Helping them to improve their self-image and develop social skills may enable them to start to break the cycle (Fig 7.1).

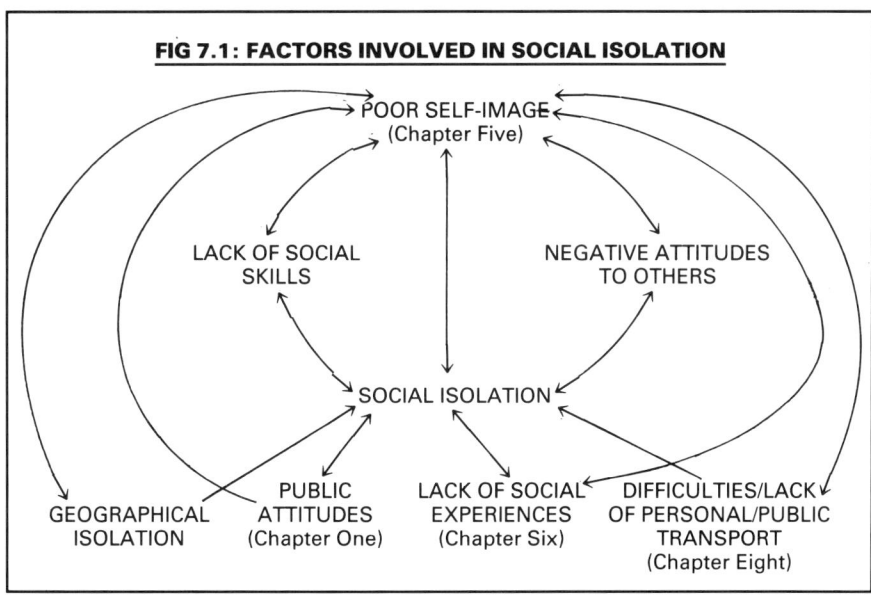

RELATIONSHIPS WITH PARENTS

It is important to highlight a major area of difficulty which many parents and their children face in their children's fight for independence. The transition from child to adult can be painful for any family but often this process can be harder for families with a disabled child. Many parents invest a great deal of time and energy into the care of their disabled child to the point that their identity can become defined through their caring role. As one mother phrased it:

> "Trying to be very honest with myself, I have decided that I actually need Edward far more than he needs me. He is my crutch. Having spent all these years encouraging him to be as independent as possible within his capabilities, I don't really like it, that he needs me less than I need him".
> J Davies (ASBAH Link Magazine)

The implications of this common process for disabled young people is that they may not only have to battle with their own needs and feelings about becoming more independent, but also with those of their well-intentioned but protective parents. The process of becoming independent will be made easier if young people are equipped with the relevant relationship skills.

RELATIONSHIPS WITH PROFESSIONALS

Many carers, eg. residential care staff and non-teaching assistants, also invest a great deal of time and energy into disabled young people in their care. This can lead to ambivalence for some carers working towards developing independence in students with disabilities on the one hand and on the other, wanting disabled young people to be dependent on them possibly to fulfil their own needs for dependent children. This can prevent their seeing if and when they are no longer needed. Some LEAs inadvertently discourage carers who help students to become independent, by taking away their jobs. In other words, in some LEAs, carers who encourage independence, work themselves out of employment. Although relationships training with students with disabilities can do little to change this situation, students can learn to assert when they need help and when they do not.

Furthermore, it is vital to re-emphasise that the structural iatrogenesis outlined in Chapter One is all too often a prime feature of relationships between service providers and young people with disabilities. Thus, if young people with disabilities could develop the relationship skills outlined in this chapter, their perception of the roles of professionals as all-knowing experts would change to a more balanced view and the negative aspects of their relationships with professionals could be minimised.

Having outlined the need to develop relationship skills, how can this be done?

Many aspects of the holographic model of living skills are applicable to developing and maintaining successful relationships and are covered throughout the book. Most particularly, the skills and attitudes involved in Developing the Self are prerequisites to developing and maintaining fulfilling relationships with others: it is very difficult to respect, value and accept others unless one respects, values and accepts oneself. The skills specifically covered here are:

- Assertiveness
- Communication Skills
- Giving and Receiving Feedback
- Asking for and Rejecting Help
- Managing Conflict
- Ending Relationships

Taken together the above skills will be called "Relationship Skills Training".

CONCEPTS UNDERLYING SKILL DEVELOPMENT

Before looking at each skill in more depth, it is important to establish some concepts which underlie the development of all these skills, namely Genuineness, Respect, Empathy and Appropriateness.

Genuineness

This is the ability to convey to others that one is authentic, can be trusted and is sincere. In essence, it is the ability to be in touch with one's own thoughts and feelings, and communicate these when it seems appropriate.

Respect

This is the ability to convey to others that they are important and valuable, and worthy of positive regard and caring. This stems from a respect for oneself.

Empathy

This is the ability to convey that one has as full an understanding as possible of the way in which another person views herself and the world. This stems from one being secure enough in one's own identity to be able to move into another person's world without the fear of being overwhelmed by it.

Appropriateness

This is the ability to judge what and how much to disclose to whom, where and when.

A person-centred approach to relationship skills training requires a climate which reflects genuineness, respect and empathic understanding. This means that trainers should demonstrate these qualities towards each other and the students, and should encourage students to convey the same qualities. It is also essential to underline the importance of appropriateness when conveying thoughts, feelings and/or information to others. These four characteristics are the basis for developing and maintaining all relationships: without them, the specific skills outlined in the rest of this chapter are less valuable.

ASSERTIVENESS

Before outlining the meaning of assertiveness and the purpose of assertiveness training, we will consider the difference between assertiveness, aggression and non-assertiveness (see Fig 7.2).

FIG 7.2: THE DIFFERENCE BETWEEN ASSERTION, AGGRESSION AND NON-ASSERTION

Assertion	*Aggression*	*Non-Assertion*
YOU DO:	YOU DO:	YOU DO:
*ask for what you want, directly, openly and appropriately	*try to get what you want in any way that works, often giving rise to bad feelings in others	*hope that you will get what you want
*have rights	*threaten, cajole, manipulate, use sarcasm, fight	*sit on feelings
*ask confidently and without undue anxiety		*rely on others to guess what you want
YOU DON'T:	YOU DON'T:	YOU DON'T:
*violate other people's rights	*respect that other people have a right to have their needs met	*ask for what you want
*expect other people to magically know what you want	*look for situations in which you both might be able to get what you want ("win-win situations")	*express your feelings
*freeze up with anxiety		*usually get what you want
		*upset anyone
		*get noticed

Adapted from:
Lifeskills Teaching Programmes No. 1
Page 118, Hopson and Scally
Lifeskills Associates 1981

As implied above, the word assertiveness may conjure up images of aggression and stubbornness, refusal to do anything suggested by adults. These images are false in three ways: first, assertiveness is the antithesis of aggression, brashness, irrational and unreasonable behaviour. Secondly, the images do a disservice to young people by assuming that, given a choice, they will rebel against staff's suggestions for no good reason. If staff facilitate young people to gain their own sense of control, the majority will listen to reason. The minority who won't probably need to rebel against authority anyway. The skills of assertiveness may not affect them one way or the other or they could temper the rebellion so that it is less self-destructive. Finally, these misconceptions about assertiveness do a disservice to professionals, as they imply that advice given may not be worthy of being heard for its own sake.

Assertiveness refers to the appropriate expression of positive and negative feelings and thoughts. The main prerequisites to assertiveness are a positive self-image, a belief in oneself (see page **54**) and a knowledge of one's rights (see page **80**). The skills of assertiveness enable us to ask for what we need and want appropriately, directly, honestly, confidently and without undue anxiety.

One of the inhibiting factors to independence in terms of self-care was identified as passivity (Table 3.1). Assertiveness training will help young people with disabilities to develop the skills necessary to overcome this barrier. If they learn to state their disability and their needs without feeling guilty or ashamed, they will be in a better position to ensure that their needs are met and simultaneously earn the respect of others.

Although there are a few pastoral care staff in ordinary schools and a few educational pyschologists and counsellors working in both ordinary and special schools who offer assertiveness training to disabled young people, the great majority of schools do not offer it. However, assertiveness training with adults is a growing field as reflected in the number of adult training colleges now offering it, and the increasing volume of literature on the subject (Dickson 1986). A further example and more specifically, the Women's Therapy Centre in London offers assertiveness training courses for women with disabilities. We recommend that these courses, or adapted versions of them, should be offered to younger disabled people within schools. Many assertiveness skills are the same as those featured elsewhere in this book, examples are decision-making skills (see page **58**) and the skills of self-reflection (see page **76**).

Assertiveness is an integral part of empowerment. It can be developed through the hidden curriculum by, for instance, involving students in the design of the living skills curriculum and their individual programmes, and it can be developed through explicit assertiveness training courses.

COMMUNICATION SKILLS

Communication skills relate to the use of verbal and non-verbal behaviours. Communication is a process of sending and receiving messages in the form of speech, signs or Blissymbols and the "non-verbal" behaviours including eye contact, facial expressions and body movements.

Sending messages involves knowing what one wants to communicate, then choosing methods of sending the information. With effective communication skills, young people become better at choosing when, where and how they communicate messages. The main skills involved in sending messages are keeping the message simple and monitoring the response of the receiver. Receiving messages involves the skills of active listening which implies listening to the content in the words and the feelings behind them. Sometimes, we are inclined to hear what we want to hear rather than what is actually stated. It is helpful to keep this in mind when listening to others, particularly if we have a vested interest in the statement or response which the communicator is making.

Young people with verbal communication difficulties should have access to speech therapists, who are the most appropriate professionals to assess the type and extent of speech impairments. They can also recommend the most useful aids or adaptations. Young people with speech impairments can also work out their own informal systems of communication with their peers. For example, some students use the first letter of words to start their communication.

The biggest handicap experienced by people with speech impairments is other people's awkwardness. Many able-bodied people feel embarrassed if they cannot understand someone else's speech, and hesitate in asking them to repeat themselves. Some people will finish sentences for someone with a speech impairment, guessing what she is trying to say. Although some young people with communication difficulties may find this helpful to speed up the communication process sometimes, it is essential that they feel able to correct someone who has made a wrong guess. Furthermore, it is important to recognise and respect that some young people find it intrusive and offensive if others finish their sentences for them. Thus, dealing with other people's awkwardness and developing the patience to repeat statements, and the skills of assertiveness are particularly important for those with communication difficulties.

Given the stigma attached to alternative forms of communication, it may also be helpful if other young people learn the basics of these systems, for instance Blissymbols: this could be fun and they may become more sensitive to the difficulties experienced by those who use them. They may also learn the variety of ways of communicating and the importance of non-verbal communication. Although this is applicable to students in all schools, it is arguably especially valuable for able-bodied children in integrated settings. Furthermore, whenever possible, it is helpful for young people with verbal communication difficulties to maximise their non-verbal communication skills, eg. use of facial expressions, body positioning. However, it is recognised that some young people with severe physical disabilities may not be able to control their body sufficiently in order to control, in turn, the non-verbal messages they give out. In general, young people with disabilities should be encouraged to develop their verbal and non-verbal communication skills to the best of their ability.

GIVING AND RECEIVING FEEDBACK

Able-bodied people are likely to display bizarre behaviours in interactions with people with disabilities, (Hollin 1986). Therefore, young people with disabilities often do not receive everyday feedback from able-bodied people which relates to them as individuals but rather to their disability. Thus, young people with disabilities, in particular, can benefit greatly from learning how to receive more realistic, individualised feedback. If students learn the skills of giving constructive feedback, they can help each other to learn. Feedback can also reveal as much about the giver as the recipient. For instance, the giver of the feedback is likely to highlight the attributes of the recipient which she thinks are most important. Thus, giving feedback also offers opportunities for learning about oneself.

Constructive feedback by professionals gives students the opportunity to change their behaviour by enhancing their self-awareness. Some forms of feedback are already commonplace within schools, such as giving praise, written comments on homework. Constructive feedback can be positive and/or negative. Constructive negative feedback leaves an individual with skills to work on, while destructive negative feedback leaves a person feeling badly about herself. Positive feedback is generally easier to receive except when it causes embarrassment, because accepting praise is seen as arrogant or boastful, and value is generally placed on humility. It is necessary to learn to know when we have done a good job and to be pleased with appropriate praise. People often forget to give each other positive feedback, taking others' positive assets for granted. If these barriers can be overcome, then the benefits to self-esteem can be enormous.

There are times when it may not be appropriate to give negative feedback, particularly when an individual is distressed. However, in general, the maximum benefit is accrued with the judicious use of a balance of positive and negative feedback, with feedback starting with positive statements and moving on to areas to be improved. Statements should be made sensitively, clearly and specifically, as soon after the event as possible.

It is ineffective either to avoid giving negative feedback or to skirt around the issues out of pity as this does not give the receiver the opportunity to learn or improve. Instead, it is important to make one or two comments at any given time, focusing on specific behaviours which are feasible to change, and offering suggestions of ways to do so. Negative feedback should be comment, not condemnation. It is better to make the statement from one's own point of view, for example, "you seemed to me to lack confidence in that situation", rather than the less helpful and inaccurate "you lack confidence". Once the feedback is given, one should check that the receiver realises it is her behaviour that is being criticised, not her worth as a human being. It is important that the environment in which the feedback is given is safe enough that the receiver feels able to be open to it rather than defensive. This is particularly so if the feedback has a negative component. Once the receiver has listened to the feedback, checked that what she heard was the same as what was said, asked for other people's opinions and possibly asked for some further specific feedback, it is ultimately her decision on whether or how to use the feedback, and if so, the way to use it most effectively. In other words, feedback is suggestive rather than instructive.

GIVING AND RECEIVING, ASKING FOR AND REJECTING HELP

Many young people with disabilities are used to receiving practical help, most of which is essential. However, there may be times when they could do more for themselves. The skills of Maintenance time (see page **97**) should enable them to minimise their physical dependency on others. The skills of assertiveness can enable young people to reject help when it is imposed on them and they feel it is not needed. Staff too, need assertiveness skills and the ability to differentiate between needed and unneeded help. There is sometimes a conflict between other people's needs and the needs of the individual with a disability. It is important that young people do negotiate for help, asking and learning to accept that sometimes other people are busy and cannot help immediately. Whilst it is recognised that this can be difficult within the dynamics of a family or the classroom, good relating skills and self-confidence can help young people to start to find this balance.

Young people with disabilities are often denied the opportunities to give to others, especially when they are seen as "unfortunate recipients" of care. If young people can define and assert how they would like to help others in any given situation and be encouraged to do so, they open up new opportunities for relating. On an individual level, this could mean students sharing skills. For instance, one student who is good at maths and less mobile helps another student with maths and in turn is offered mobility assistance. On a wider scale, students could be encouraged to participate in organised events. Examples are raising money for voluntary sector services or volunteering in community service projects with other members of the community.

MANAGING CONFLICT IN RELATIONSHIPS

Managing conflict within relationships, disagreeing with or having an argument with someone who is a close friend can be difficult for anyone. It has been suggested that this can be particularly difficult for girls and young women (Orbach and Eichenbaum 1988). Anecdotal evidence suggests that young people with disabilities who need personal care assistance face an additional dimension to managing conflict within relationships: if an individual is reliant on other people for certain aspects of her physical care, she takes more risks in bringing up an argument with an adult or a peer, as she might believe that the care would be withdrawn. It is less important whether this is the actual situation or not; it is the young person's perception of the situation which is important. Research is needed to explore this theory.

The skills of managing conflict within relationships stem from a positive self-image and the skills of managing emotions (see page **61**). The relationship skills outlined so far in this chapter are essentially the same as those involved in managing conflict within relationships, ie. skills of communication and assertiveness.

ENDING RELATIONSHIPS

When relationships between people end, the effects can be devastating. There is no reason to suppose that this is less true for adolescents. In fact, it may be worse as they often have less experience to draw on to help them cope. It is important that young people are aware that when relationships end, it does not mean they have failed. Furthermore, it is important to empathise with the pain involved, and to confirm that the pain does lessen with time and it is possible to develop other relationships.

RELATIONSHIP SKILLS TRAINING

Relationship skills within the framework outlined can be developed through structured programmes. Although the details of these programmes are beyond the scope of this book, the two main training techniques used will be outlined briefly – **role-playing** and **modelling**. Both techniques should be accompanied by feedback, and video-tape recorders can be useful to provide immediate feedback. Role-playing is often the most essential tool for relationship skills training. This technique enables young people to enact brief scenes which simulate real-life situations, eg. role-plays of ending relationships and managing conflict within relationships. In this way, they have the opportunity to test new behaviours in a safe, empowering environment.

The acquisition of relationship skills is partly based on observation and imitation of persons who are meaningful to the student (Bandura 1977). Thus training programmes often use either live or filmed models. The effectiveness of modelling will depend on a number of factors (Gresham 1981): first, the young person needs to be sufficiently motivated to concentrate on the model. Second, she needs to be able to identify with the model. This would imply that models with visible physical disabilities would be more effective than able-bodied models. The models should not be so competent in displaying the behaviour that they intimidate the observers. Finally, the observer needs to be able to remember the model's behaviour and be able to imitate it.

Relationships are what living is about. Helping disabled young people to appropriately develop, maintain and end relationships is an essential aspect of becoming empowered. Thus, it should be an integral part of any living skills curriculum.

CHAPTER EIGHT
Working and Playing

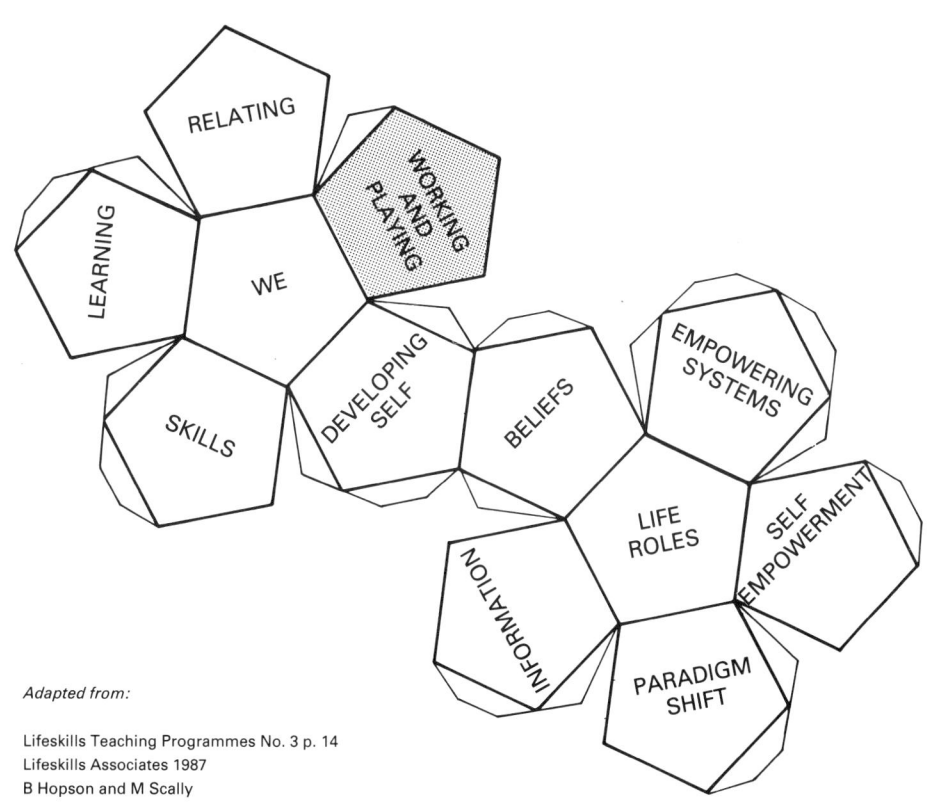

Adapted from:

Lifeskills Teaching Programmes No. 3 p. 14
Lifeskills Associates 1987
B Hopson and M Scally

WORKING AND PLAYING

This chapter considers the broad areas of the holographic model described as working and playing. For ease of discussion, these have been subdivided into time management skills, maintenance skills, leisure time skills and sold time skills (see Fig 3.2). These skills are not mutually exclusive – indeed some directly overlap, such as leisure time activities which can take the form of exercise and thus be beneficial to health management. These concepts of time were first outlined by Jack Loughary (1977). For the purposes of this book, they have been slightly adapted and linked to skill acquisition. Time management skills have been given elevated status here since they are essential to young people with disabilities for reasons which are explained later in the chapter.

It can appear that the division of "working and playing" into four skill areas is another exercise in introducing jargon. However, this framework gives a clear, simple picture of the way people spend their time, and offers a valuable way to help people establish priorities so they can lead a lifestyle of their choice. Without this, there is a danger that many young people with severe physical disabilities may end up spending a disproportionate amount of their adult lives on maintenance time skills, almost by default, without considering or prioritising other options for "working and playing".

TIME MANAGEMENT

To learn to manage and use time more effectively, we first need to become aware of how we presently use our time and identify priorities. These priorities should then be ranked in order of importance and a distinction made between priorities within sold time, leisure time and maintenance time (Hopson and Scally 1981). From this base-line we can begin to identify changes we wish to make.

The statement "we haven't got the time" can mean "we haven't got clear priorities". Managing time effectively must include time for relaxation so that we have more energy for gaining maximum benefit from working and playing, learning and relating to others – it does not refer to filling in every moment of every day.

There is no objective measure of importance for choosing priorities as this is individual and variable. Thus, time-wasting is a value judgement based on the individuals' objectives and priorities. This implies that however strongly you may feel that a student is wasting her time, it is her decision how she uses that time, unless she is causing you to waste your time or she is not attending classes/sessions to which she is committed.

There are strong arguments for suggesting that young people with disabilities have even greater need for time-management skills than their able-bodied peers: many need to spend considerable time learning and performing maintenance tasks that able-bodied young people accomplish with relative ease. Even if they need a personal care assistant and can organise and direct her efficiently, young people with disabilities often still need more time to conduct these tasks. For example, when it might take two or three minutes for an able-bodied person to go to the toilet, for many young people with disabilities, even with efficient management it may take 10 to 15 minutes. Furthermore, young people with disabilities are even more likely than their able-bodied peers to spend their leisure time doing passive activities (see page **123**). This is partly because they have less access to more active leisure opportunities. Some may themselves consider that continuously watching television is a waste of their time. Identifying priorities and desires could be the first step to engaging in more leisure time pursuits.

Finally, young people with progressive conditions may find that they are physically unable to spend time doing the things they used to prioritise. The skills of management are one tool to enable them to re-examine their lives and change their priorities to suit their current needs.

MAINTENANCE TIME SKILLS

Maintenance time skills are the skills of everyday living, namely self-care skills, health management skills, mobility skills and home management skills (see Fig 8.1). These are the tasks which are generally covered under the auspices of "self-care and independence" training. As has already become clear, becoming more independent as defined in this book demands more than the acquisition of these skills. In this context, it is important to state clearly that what is currently often seen as "self-care and independence training" should be recognised as "maintenance time training", and to make distinctions between this and the wider view of independence training adopted here.

In 1983, Bookis found that young people with disabilities were not learning maintenance time skills as many schools were not teaching these skills as an integrated part of their curricula. Has anything changed? During the current research, 94% of special schools and 65% of ordinary schools which responded to the postal questionnaire stated that they had a policy on "self-care and independence" training. The largest percentage of schools with no such policy were ordinary schools operating a policy of full integration. 59% of special schools and 17% of ordinary schools had documented this policy or their practice in facilitating the development of these skills. These figures may be an over-estimate as we cannot know whether schools focusing on these skills were more likely to have responded to the questionnaire.

FIG 8.1: MAINTENANCE TIME SKILLS

Self-Care Skills	Health Management	Mobility Skills	Home Management
Eating & drinking	Nutrition	Indoor skills	Shopping and money management
Bathing/showering	Exercise	Outdoor skills	In the kitchen
Hair care	Prevention of pressure sores	Maintaining and stowing aids	In the bedroom
Dressing, clothing & footwear	Medication	Transport	Light cleaning
Coping with menstruation	National Health Service		Safety
Incontinence management	Using alternative medicine		

The results indicate a marked difference between the number of ordinary schools compared to special schools, which have a policy on facilitating the development of these skills. Why is this? When visiting many of the ordinary schools, the researchers were told that by the time students with disabilities commenced secondary school at 11, they were able to conduct most maintenance time tasks to the best of their ability, so there was no need for training. However, the data does not support this assertion and without stringent assessment procedures, it is difficult to know how schools can make it with any validity (see page **142**). The Association for Spina Bifida and Hydrocephalus has found that many ordinary schools were misinformed about the level of physical independence students had already achieved. The anecdotal evidence found in this study suggests that this situation still exists in ordinary schools.

Some ordinary schools, whilst recognising the need for this training, argue that they do not have the time to introduce it into an already crowded curriculum (Trend and Nicoll 1987). But if young people are to become independent in their adult lives, they must be taught maintenance skills. There has to be an emphasis on individual needs and priorities. For example, is it more important to be able to manage incontinence or learn the rudiments of French?

TABLE 8.1: THE NUMBER OF SCHOOLS WITH PARAMEDICAL SUPPORT

	Number of Therapists					
	Speech Therapist		Occupational Therapist		Physiotherapist	
	≥1	<1	≥1	<1	≥1	<1
Ordinary Schools (LEA) (n = 35)	3	8	10	11	25	10
Special Schools (Private) (n = 11)	6	3	4	1	10	1
Mainstream Schools (n = 23)	1	4	–	3	3	9

Key

Total number of schools (n) = 69
Number of LEA special schools (n) = 35
Number of private special schools (n) = 11
Number of ordinary schools (n) = 23

≥ = Greater than or equivalent to one full-time therapist.
< = At least two hours per week and less than one full-time therapist or the equivalent.

NB *The categories "Speech Therapist", "Occupational Therapist" and "Physiotherapist" are not mutually exclusive.*

Although it may not be appropriate for ordinary schools with a few children with disabilities to have a full-time occupational therapist, speech therapist or physiotherapist, all schools should have access to their advice and input when required if they are to teach these skills. For example, occupational therapists have the knowledge to ensure that young people are sitting at a table of the correct height and in a chair which gives them effective support. They address perceptual difficulties, hand function activities and fine motor activities to minimise the effects of various impairments and give advice on appropriate equipment.

The results of this study show that ordinary schools have less access to paramedical support than special schools (Table 8.1), even though some of the ordinary schools with units cater for as many children with physical disabilities as some of the special schools. This is possibly due to a lack of liaison between health, education, medical and social services.

This relative lack of paramedical support could be one reason why facilitating the development of maintenance time skills is not prioritised within the ordinary schools as compared with special schools. It is essential to determine how much this lack of resources affects the ability of young people with disabilities to succeed in the integrated system. The overall picture within special schools is very different with the majority having adequate paramedical support. Maintenance time skills are usually given an elevated status in working towards independence, often to the exclusion of other skills which can enable young people to become more self-empowered. To reiterate, the holographic model describes a multi-faceted process in which no one aspect is accorded greater importance.

Maintenance time skills must be taught with reference to the home environment. Wherever possible, staff should conduct home visits so that they can ensure that skills taught at school can be used at home. Where this is not feasible, schools might consider designing a questionnaire for parents asking for relevant basic information, such as a questionnaire about the bathroom or kitchen (see Appendix 3).

These skills can be boring to learn, so some schools have found it helpful to use an awards scheme to help motivate students (see Appendix 5). The advantages and disadvantages of this scheme are the same as those for the Royal Society for the Prevention of Accidents (RoSPA) mobility awards which are discussed later in this chapter (see page **117**).

It is important to bear in mind, when teaching maintenance time skills, that there is a difference between a young person learning to direct another to perform a task and a young person needing to learn how and when to perform a task herself. However, the results from the structured interview schedule used in this study show that young people and their parents did not see this difference. It suggests that schools are not stressing the difference and are not encouraging young people to direct a carer when this is appropriate for those who are, and always will be, physically unable to do a task.

SELF-CARE

It is essential that young people learn self-care skills to enable them to become more independent. Intervention should start pre-school with parents and children together so that by 11, children have already developed some of the skills outlined here (eg. Feldman and Varni 1982). This section focuses on the skills of eating and drinking, bathing, hair care and dressing, and for girls, how to cope with menstruation, and for those with incontinence problems, the skills of incontinence management. At the end of this section, some of the issues involved in giving intimate care to young people with disabilities are raised.

Eating and Drinking

Some young people with disabilities take longer to eat a meal than their peers, so heat-retaining plates can be helpful. Food should be presented in a form which enables young people to be as physically independent as possible, eg. a salad sandwich rather than bread, butter and salad. They should also have access to advice from speech therapists and occupational therapists about body positioning, positioning of utensils, eating/drinking techniques and any equipment they need such as angled or padded cutlery, two-handled mugs, adapted table and/or chair. Some may need protective clothing so they do not make their clothes dirty, for instance aprons or napkins, but young people should not be made to wear a bib. For those who may spill liquids when drinking, an absorbent apron may be more appropriate (ie. an apron with towelling on the front and plastic on the back), so that they can protect themselves properly, rather than have to take luke-warm instead of hot drinks.

Young people with disabilities who need personal care assistance to eat and drink should have as much choice as possible: choosing what food on the plate they eat, the order in which they eat it, when they sip a drink and the rate at which they eat. It is possible to facilitate these choices with young people with the most severe multiple impairments, by asking them to point to the item they next wish to eat or drink.

Within ordinary schools, young people who need personal care assistance or who feed themselves in an unusual way should be able to choose whether or not they eat with their able-bodied peers. Neither compulsory segregation nor integration is satisfactory as one person may find eating in front of peers embarrassing whilst another with the same disability may wish to eat with friends. Behavioural self-care checklists are frequently used in special schools and less often in ordinary schools. The social acceptability of the manner in which one eats is an issue for those working within the special and integrated school system. The "feeding" section of these checklists usually has a sub-division called "appropriate table manners". Young people with disabilities have as much right to these manners as anyone else so that they can become more easily integrated into society. But it is important that if a child or young person is being encouraged to eat in a certain way purely for the sake of etiquette, this reason should be communicated to them. It is potentially destructive to present a child's problem as individual when the problem is essentially societal. The sub-division of the checklists promotes the idea that young people who eat in an unusual way or who have not absorbed these manners have an individual pathology, rather than a problem arising from society's requirements. Therefore, in the light of the mass of maintenance time skills which young people with disabilities need to cover, it is suggested that this sub-division of the checklists should be reviewed by each school and withdrawn.

Bathing/Showering

The study results show that 66% of parents thought their children could bathe/shower without help compared with 55% of young people themselves (see Table 8.2). This indicates that some parents perceived their children to be more physically able than do the young people themselves. There was no difference between the results from the initial and final interviews.

TABLE 8.2: BATHING AND SHOWERING PRACTICE AT INITIAL INTERVIEW

	Percentage of Responses	
	Young People	*Parents*
	%	%
WITHOUT ASSISTANCE	55	66
WITH ASSISTANCE	45	34

Key
Total number of parents (n) = 36
Total number of young people (n) = 36

Young people with mobility difficulties need to develop their own bathing/showering routines so that they become as physically independent as possible. To do this, they need time to try out different methods and need access to advice from occupational therapists and physiotherapists regarding body positioning and equipment or adaptations such as bath boards or bath inserts. Although bathing routines are helpful, young people may wish to adapt them according to their mood.

Young people who have loss of or incomplete sensations in their legs should learn ways to appreciate the temperature of their bath/shower to avoid the possibility of scalding. Some occupational therapists advise using a thermometer while others suggest using the elbow or another part of the body to check temperature.

Young people who are physically unable to bathe/shower without personal care assistance should be taught to direct a carer so that they can bathe/shower in the way that they wish. Young people whose conditions are deteriorating need to re-examine their needs with adequate paramedical support. Short, residential "independence" courses have been found to be effective in enabling young people to develop bathing routines as improvements appear to last over time (Macredie and Bradshaw 1984).

Hair Care

Hair care involves basic washing to keep it clean and maintain it in good condition. The study results indicate that some young people learned to wash their hair without personal care assistance during the two-term duration of the study (Table 8.3).

TABLE 8.3: WASHING HAIR PRACTICE

	Percentage of Responses			
	Initial Interview		Final Interview	
	Young People	*Parents*	*Young People*	*Parents*
	%	%	%	%
WITHOUT ASSISTANCE	42	44	56	50
WITH ASSISTANCE	58	56	44	50

Key
Total number of parents (n) = 36
Total number of young people (n) = 36

Of those who required assistance, approximately 50% said "Mum or Dad do it" – and this did not change between the first and third interviews. This could imply that young people were not learning to wash their own hair at home regardless of what was happening at school, and/or that facilities at home were unsuitable for independent hair washing.

Hair care goes beyond the need for basic cleanliness. It is equally important that young people with disabilities have access to the same fashionable hair styles as their peers. Thus, some schools and short "independence" courses have introduced hair dressing and fashion into their programmes which is designed to act in the way that fashionable peer pressure acts in an ordinary school.

Dressing, Clothing and Footwear

A substantial proportion of young people with disabilities need personal care assistance when dressing (Table 8.4). Although there was a marked increase in the number of students who said that they could dress without assistance at the end of the study, this was not what their parents said.

All children learn the skills of undressing before they learn the skills of dressing. It takes the average able-bodied child until the age of eight years old

TABLE 8.4: DRESSING SKILLS

	Percentage of Responses			
	Initial Interview		Final Interview	
	Young People	Parents	Young People	Parents
	%	%	%	%
WITHOUT ASSISTANCE	61	61	75	64
WITH ASSISTANCE	39	39	25	36

Key
Total number of parents (n) = 36
Total number of young people (n) = 36

to be totally physically independent in dressing including being able to identify garments. The process of dressing is a complex exercise requiring the co-ordination of multiple motor, sensory and neurological responses, including the following:

- a reasonably accurate body image
- tactile senses
- choosing and recognising the required items from a pile of clothes
- working out which way round clothes go
- recognising head, arm and leg holes and the parts of the body to put in them
- maintaining balance
- high manual dexterity to manipulate fastenings.

For young people with multiple disabilities, including perceptual and/or learning difficulties, the many dressing procedures are extremely difficult. Indeed, dressing is a microcosm of all other maintenance time activities and could serve as a gauge for progress in all of them. Pinpointing the areas of greatest difficulty within individual programmes, may help young people and their carers to determine the extent of the disability and the ways if any, in which they can be overcome (see page **141**).

Looking good can help people feel good so improving self-confidence and self-esteem. Each person's clothing reflects the image she wants to present to others. It is important that young people with disabilities develop their own individual style by choosing their own clothes which will usually be ones in current fashion. They should be encouraged to choose clothing styles that also suit their individual needs, eg. with large buttons or easily accessible zips. Simple adaptations can sometimes make dressing a lot easier, eg. changing the fastenings.

Some young people may prefer to wear clothes that have been significantly adapted or made to meet their individual needs, eg. young people who use appliances to manage incontinence difficulties may have clothes made or adapted to enable them to empty their appliances without getting undressed. Young people who spend the day sitting may find that trousers hang better if they are made with a higher back and a lower front. Information on altering regular clothing patterns is available from the Disabled Living Foundation, and it may be possible to get help from a local technical college or local dressmakers. There are also a number of organisations which adapt and make clothes, eg. Fashion Services for the Disabled. However, some young people prefer to wear ordinary clothes because of the social stigma attached to adapted clothing.

It is important to wear appropriate footwear to increase mobility and/or reduce the risk of pressure sores. Orthopaedic and surgical footwear are available from hospitals but since these are often ugly, in some health authorities it may be possible for young people to design their own footwear. However, since this is unusual, many young people wear "trainers". The Disabled Living Foundation has information about trainers which can be adapted for use with calipers. Ultimately, it is each individual's choice as to the clothes and shoes they wish to wear assuming that they have information about the options available and can make an informed choice taking both fashion and comfort into account.

Young people with disabilities should be taught how to make a decision about when they need clean clothes. Fifty per cent of the young people interviewed said they did this and a further 14% made the decision jointly with their parents or carers. They should also be taught the skills of washing clothes, to enable them to live more independently in later life. However, it is recognised that few young people volunteer to wash clothes if their parents are willing to do it. Twenty-two per cent of young people interviewed said that they had washed some clothes in the months prior to the first interview whilst 28% reported that they had done this in the month prior to the last interview. Young people should be taught the importance of having a clean sheet and mattress changed if either become soiled.

Although teaching young people to iron and mend clothes may be useful, it is not considered an essential part of a self-care programme for young people aged 10–16 years.

Menstruation

Of those girls who had started their periods, 75% said that they could change their sanitary protection without assistance, but only 66% of parents thought their child could do this. Since menstruation is a sign of womanhood, this discrepancy may reflect the difficulties that some parents face when their children become more independent (see page **157**).

Whilst some young people with paralysis of the lower part of the body may experience less abdominal discomfort, others may experience more because they are sedentary. For those who are incontinent, menstruation may be more complicated on both physical and emotional levels. Since girls with Spina Bifida are likely to mature physically earlier than most females, the onset of menstruation may cause emotional difficulties.

Girls with disabilities should be taught the skills of self-care during menstruation and have access to counselling if appropriate.

Incontinence Management

Urinary incontinence is defined as the inappropriate involuntary passage of urine resulting in wetting.

Faecal incontinence is defined as the inability to control bowel movements.

Young people may be incontinent either because their impairments directly affect the bladder as in Spina Bifida, or because they cannot manage to use the lavatory. They are likely to experience considerable social stigma, and may acquire secondary medical problems such as urinary infections or kidney damage, unless they can manage their incontinence appropriately. The study results show a discrepancy between the answers of parents and their children suggesting that some young people are unable to manage their incontinence without active assistance or direction (Table 8.5).

These results are consistent with the findings of Parker (1984) highlighting a gap in communication about incontinence training between parents and schools.

TABLE 8.5: MANAGEMENT OF BLADDER AND BOWELS

	Percentage of Responses			
	Initial Interview		Final Interview	
	Young People	*Parents*	*Young People*	*Parents*
	%	%	%	%
WITHOUT ASSISTANCE	72	66	81	75
WITH ASSISTANCE	23	22	11	19
WITH DIRECTION	6	11	8	6

Both those who have urinary incontenence and their parents should be trained in the management of appliances, eg. taught the skills of self-catheterisation. Simple gadgets, eg. a bleeper or an alarm sound on a wristwatch, can serve to remind young people to go to the toilet. Their use is to stop "constant nagging" by a member of staff to check bags or appliances. Incontinence management can be made easier if young people wear clothes which are easier to cope with (see page **103**). Schools should provide sufficient space and privacy to enable them to practise these skills. Young people should know how to organise their own supplies and/or what to do if their appliances are inadequate for them. Both those who have faecal incontinence and their parents, should receive instruction in "self-help" skills, eg. using suppositories or reflex anal response.

Those who are embarrassed or ashamed of their incontinence should be supported by staff and have access to counselling, if needed. Some young people may be ashamed of their incontinence and it is essential that staff do not show disgust or other negative reactions which might reinforce their shame and be mimicked by other students. The following case history from an ordinary school illustrates how the attitudes of staff were changed towards a boy and the subsequent improvements both in relationships and in the boy's management of his incontinence.

> '"Jonathan" is 14 years old. He has Spina Bifida and is paralysed from the waist down. He is confined to a wheelchair and is doubly incontinent.
>
> Since Jonathan first came to the school 3 years ago, he has caused the care staff considerable problems. He often arrived at school dirty and dishevelled, and was often wet. Various attempts at helping him manage his incontinence seemed to have failed, and staff had fallen into a routine of criticising or nagging him, or showing resigned acceptance – "Oh well, he's a typical Spina Bifida, isn't he!"'
>
> This year, as Jonathan reached puberty, we began to despair that he would never be concerned that his main school friends might find him smelly and wet. He is an extremely affable young man who gets on well with adults and his peers, yet we felt that his physical appearance was being less tolerated.
>
> At one of our staff meetings, we sat and analysed our attitude to Jonathan and decided to adopt a much more positive approach. One of the care staff "volunteered" to oversee Jonathan's progress and help with his learning programme.
>
> The first step was to find out why he was so often wet.
> – was it pure laziness? – not going to check his bag at break times.
> – was his urinary appliance working properly?
> – did he know how to check his appliance?
> – were there any particular times during the day/week when Jonathan was wet?

On discussion later it was observed that Jonathan was actually going to check his bag at fairly regular intervals, but . . .
1. He often failed to do up the tap again once he had emptied his bag!
2. If his pouch came loose, he thought a "good pat" would seal it again!
3. Certain physical activities, such as hydrotherapy and falling out of his chair loosened his pouch.

We next planned a carefully structured, step-by-step programme. Our emphasis was to make Jonathan succeed, and to find all possible ways to praise him rather than criticize.

At first, his member of the care staff went to help at his request if he found he was wet. This way it was possible to teach Jonathan how to attach a new pouch properly and check his appliance thoroughly each time.

To help Jonathan's organisation and memory, he had to tick a book every time (four times a day) he checked his bag, and if he was wet, he had to explain why.

We used Jonathan's love of food and drink as a reward. After a good week, he had a cup of coffee made for him by a member of staff.

Success! Jonathan now fills up a book twice a day (we still feel he needs this reminder), is rarely wet, and is still enjoying his Friday coffee.

Short courses seem to be effective in enabling young people to sort out immediate practical problems of incontinence. However, when effective intervention needs to be on a long-term basis, the short courses, by definition, cannot hope to deal fully with the emotional and social problems associated with incontinence.

STAFF ISSUES CONCERNING INTIMATE CARE PRACTICE

The amount of physical assistance some young disabled people need will result in some staff having intimate contact with young people and particularly with the parts and functions of their bodies which are generally regarded as taboo. This raises a number of issues which need to be considered.

The objective of personal care assistants should be to provide the help a young person requires while simultaneously respecting her right to privacy and dignity. Some young people with disabilities claim to be unconcerned about who sees them in situations which other people might find embarrassing. This could be a consequence of one or a combination of the following factors:
- perceiving society as having ridiculous taboos about nudity
- simple acceptance of a situation over which they believe they have no control

- seeing themselves as being asexual
- seeing their bodies unworthy of respect because of deformity or lack of sensation.

Personal care can play a major role in helping to promote an appropriate body image and behaviour thus minimising inappropriate and uninhibited behaviour in future.

Care staff and parents and others involved in providing care for disabled people should stress respect for personal privacy from an early stage so that each child learns to value it. Young people are likely to have a more balanced outlook on life if they have learnt to respect their bodies and, equally important, not be ashamed of them. There is sometimes a tendency for staff to accept a response from a young person on the lines of "I don't mind" in order to perform a task quickly. Whilst this is understandable, it is unlikely to promote self-respect and a positive self-image. This does not mean, of course, that disabled young people should be taught to be ashamed of their bodies, but that the personal care which is provided is given in such a way that if the young person "did mind" she would not find the experience uncomfortable.

The sexuality of young people needs to be recognised by personal care assistants who may be present in situations where able-bodied adolescents would normally be alone. For example, if an adolescent boy has an erection when bathing this could be embarrassing for both staff and the boy. It can be dealt with either negatively or positively. Negative ways would be to infantalise the boy and to laugh at the erection or alternatively ignore it. Both of these ignore the boys sexuality and could ultimately result in his doing the same. A more positive approach would be for staff to be able to talk to him about it openly.

The issues for girls are different but equally complex. The great majority of personal care assistants are women so most schools accept a girl's right to refuse intimate care from a man. Nevertheless, it should be recognised that women can also pass on inappropriate inhibitions either implicitly or explicitly. Adolescent girls do not normally require assistance when toiletting or bathing. Severely disabled girls however, often do and even though the care assistants are women it is important that their sexuality be respected.

The issues concerned with working with young people who have deformed bodies should also be considered. If staff perceive such people as being physically ugly they may engender negative feelings in the young people with whom they are working.

Obviously, there is no single answer to the issues raised above. Each situation will need to be dealt with differently but it would be helpful if schools or education authorities arrange staff workshops and/or support groups so that staff are able to discuss their reactions and anxieties when a particular situation arises. Some problems arise because the staff are not trained to cope with their own embarrassment.

At a policy level, schools should consider implementing a policy of male/female care which gives boys the right to refuse intimate care by a woman and vice versa. There would, however, be difficulties in implementing such a policy because of the comparatively small number of men employed as care assistants. Positive efforts should be made to recruit more men into this area of work.

HEALTH MANAGEMENT

The World Health Organisation (WHO) defines health as "the state of complete physical, mental and social well-being and not simply the absence of disease".

Although research literature shows the interactions between physical and emotional well-being and the influence of the environment on the individual, health is still usually defined within society as the absence of illness. There is also an incorrect yet common assumption that illness and disability are synonymous. This is frequently reinforced by the nature of many of the services available to people with disabilities. For example, in a short "independence" course conducted in a hospital environment, the implicit messages connect disability and illness despite explicit messages given.

Within the widely accepted and erroneous definition of health as absence of illness, young people with progressive conditions are permanently unhealthy. This view of health is detrimental to them as it is static and leaves them little room to develop.

All young people with disabilities including those with progressive conditions, should be encouraged to explore the notion of health for themselves and the various internal, social and environmental factors that affect them: they need to learn to take responsibility for their own health on an individual and a community level.

This section looks at some aspects of health management which relate to particular impairments and others which are more generalised. More specifically, it focuses on nutrition, exercise, prevention of pressure sores, medication, the National Health Service and alternative medicine. These topics do not form an exhaustive list. There is a wide range not covered here, eg. using dentists, unprescribed medication, basic first aid and broader issues like HIV and AIDS, smoking and alcohol use. These are beyond the remit of this book although they may come under the auspices of health management.

Nutrition

All schools should cover dietary training as an integral part of the school curriculum which includes teaching knowledge of the constituents of the common foods, such as the fibre, protein and mineral, carbohydrate, fat and vitamin content.

Students should learn to compare the nutritional value of a variety of fresh foods and "junk" food, so that they can see the advantages of eating well-balanced meals. They need this training if they are to make an informed choice about their present and future lifestyle.

Young people should also be informed of the content of common drinks and the importance of drinking sufficient fluids, particularly in hot weather. Young people with Spina Bifida are advised to drink at least two litres of fluid each day to reduce the risk of urinary tract infection. They should be taught the signs of infection, such as strong odour and dark colour of urine so that they are able to prevent the infection from becoming more serious.

Young people who need to be on a special diet for medical reasons, should be aware of the reasons why it is inadvisable for them to eat certain foods and be encouraged to develop a sensible eating pattern within dietary constraints. It is more helpful in the long term to encourage them to develop their own sense of responsibility and control by reasoning with them to take the decision to refuse a particular food, rather than merely imposing controls on them. It would be helpful if dinner staff could be aware of students on specific diets and the reasons for these diets. Otherwise they may unwittingly encourage students to take food which may be harmful to them.

Dietary training is usually stressed for those who are considered to be overweight. Being overweight can put undue pressure on the heart which increases the likelihood of cardiac problems in later life. In particular, young people with disabilities are often pressurised into losing weight. For those who use wheelchairs, being overweight leads to an increased likelihood of developing pressure sores. For young people with Spina Bifida and Muscular Dystrophy, it can cause the spine, already weakened, to take extra strain, sometimes resulting in spinal collapse. This can lead to scoliosis of the spine and compression of the lungs which in turn, lead to respiratory and cardiac problems. Thus, in some cases, there are medical reasons for not becoming overweight.

But what is being overweight? Being overweight could be defined as anything above our optimum weight. However, most people are unlikely to develop the medical problems outlined above unless they are obese. It is argued that many, particularly young women, including those with disabilities, are seen and see themselves as overweight in comparison to the stereotypical able-bodied image of women. For many, the stresses involved in perpetually dieting undermine the potential benefits to their health. In essence, being overweight is usually a value judgement which is more often applied to young women than young men. It is argued that being "overweight" should be considered as a valid choice (Chemin 1986).

For young people with mobility difficulties, there is an additional dimension to the issues of weight and diet. If someone is fat, she is much harder to lift and/or to push in her wheelchair. Whilst she should not be made to feel guilty about being fat, it is perfectly valid for carers to state this as one of the reasons why they suggest that she loses weight. It is much better to state this openly and sensitively than to tell her indirectly under the guise of her health. Ultimately, she must choose whether or not to endeavour to lose weight.

Exercise

Some form of exercise for young people with disabilities is essential, especially if they spend the majority of the day in a wheelchair. Lack of any exercise often leads to general mobility and movement becoming progressively slower and more difficult.

Physical education refers to activities which involve physical movement and which often give pleasure and relaxation. Although physical education is a recognised element of the school curriculum for able-bodied students, it is not always recognised as valuable for those with a physical disability. In some ordinary schools the researcher found that many disabled young people were excluded from physical education lessons. Others had found ways of involving them by adapting the lessons when appropriate, and some were offered swimming and/or physiotherapy as an alternative to the class-based games lessons. Young people with disabilities should participate in class-based lessons as much as possible.

Physical education teachers should have access to practical advice and help from physiotherapists and the medical information supplied to the schools, so alleviating any fears of involving young people with disabilities by informing them of the level of physical activity they can expect from each student.

Ordinary and special schools should offer a wide range of opportunities for exercise through the physical education curriculum. This would include adaptations of regular activities, eg. when playing football or hockey a young person using a wheelchair could be in goal and sticks or crutches could be used to "kick" the ball. Since some sports do not require adaptations, they are particularly useful in the long term as they are easier to take up after school, eg. table tennis, pool, archery, canoeing.

Non-competitive sports require no adaptations to rules as they involve the group working co-operatively to achieve a group goal, so they are good additions to the physical education curriculum. Finally, there may be room for some wheelchair sports, eg. wheelchair dancing, basketball and races.

The Prevention of Pressure Sores

Young people with restricted mobility are at risk of developing pressure sores. They are easy to prevent if young people at risk have learnt the skills of regular pressure relief and appropriate body positioning. This involves lifting the body from the wheelchair or seated position by bracing arms and holding the lift for ten seconds. This procedure should be repeated several times a day, preferably once an hour. The use of special mattresses and cushions and pressure-relieving sheepskins should be understood and it is also helpful if the basic skills of self-massage are taught. All these suggestions help restore blood circulation so helping the prevention of pressure sores.

If a person has restricted mobility, checking for signs of pressure sores should be a part of her personal care routine. Young people should be taught the skills of using mirrors to enable them to see the skin on their back, bottom, hips, elbows, feet and ankles. They should be aware that if they notice a red or grazed area on their skin, they should show it to someone. The results of this study show that only 50% of those interviewees who should check for pressure sores actually did so. Seventeen per cent said that they could do this without assistance when initially interviewed and 34% when finally interviewed. These results suggest that many young people who could benefit from checking for pressure sores were unable to do so without assistance and would routinely require this help. Moreover, there appears to be a disturbing percentage of young people who do not check at all, or who are unaware that they are being checked by school staff.

If pressure sores are allowed to develop, they are serious and difficult to heal. They affect an individual's general well-being as well as the specific area. The skin in the area of a healed pressure sore will always be more vulnerable to breakdown. Pressure sores are preventable if the procedures outlined here are regularly followed.

Medication

Young people who take regular prescribed medication should know what they take and how to obtain it. They should also know the purpose of the medication, the possible side effects and where applicable, the effects of polypharmacy (ie. the interaction of more than one drug). They should be encouraged to be totally responsible for their own medication subject to any legal restraints.

The study results show that, of those interviewees to whom the question was relevant, 41% of parents thought that their children could take their medication independently, compared to 65% of young people. These percentages are quite high given that half of them were under 14 years old. The difference in the percentages is either an indication that parents were not aware of the extent of their children's ability or, of young people overestimating their abilities.

On further questioning, it was found that 75% of young people did not know how to get more medication and/or saw it as the responsibility of a significant adult (ie. a member of care staff, school nurse or parent). This information could be provided within individual or group sessions on physical health management, conducted by the school nurse.

The National Health Service

Many young people with disabilities have substantial contact with medical professionals and the National Health Service. Thus, at a basic level, they should be aware of procedures for making appointments with general practitioners and at hospital out-patient clinics. They should know they have a right to a second opinion when seeing a general practitioner or a consultant if they wish to have more information from a particular specialist or if they feel uneasy with any advice given. They also need a knowledge of the roles of the health workers within the National Health Service, and the different types of health care available through it.

A knowledge of the nature of the Health Service and young people's rights as consumers would encourage evaluation of the service from a consumer point of view. Thus, students should be taught the purpose of Patient Participation Groups, Community Health Councils and Family Practitioner Committees. This is even more important than for their able-bodied peers because of the likelihood of increased contact with the National Health Service.

Alternative Medicine

The basic principle of holistic medicine is the recognition of nature's healing power and the body's natural ability to heal itself. There are many different therapies and techniques employed under the umbrella of holistic medicine including homeopathy and reflexology. Many are focused on prevention and some conditions may respond more favourably to one of the alternative therapies than to those of the more conventional medical model.

Young people need to be aware of the range of medical approaches available, so that they may choose the type of approach they feel would suit their individual needs at any given time. This needs to be an informed choice made on the basis of adequate information so that reputable practitioners are sought.

MOBILITY

Mobility training is part of the curriculum for both able-bodied and disabled children eg. road safety, using public transport. But young people who have mobility difficulties need additional training to enable them to move around as independently as possible. Those who use mobility aids should be trained in their use and storage. In particular, those who use wheelchairs should be taught how to transfer to and from their wheelchairs. Training should cover negotiating obstacles and using alternative forms of transport, eg. Dial-a-Ride schemes available in some areas.

Seventy-two per cent of young people interviewed in this study used mobility aids. Those used were callipers, rollators, crutches, sticks, walking frames, mobile frames, and most commonly, wheelchairs. This section is directed towards young people who use wheelchairs, giving some consideration to young people who use other mobility aids. The results show a consistent difference between perceptions of young people and their parents.

Indoor Mobility

Ninety-two per cent of young people who used mobility aids and 81% of their parents said they could use them without assistance indoors. When questioned further about the obstacles which they could negotiate indoors, the results were slightly less promising (Table 8.6). For example, by the end of

TABLE 8.6: NEGOTIATING INDOOR OBSTACLES

	Percentage who can negotiate obstacles without assistance			
	Initial Interview		Final Interview	
	Young People	Parents	Young People	Parents
	%	%	%	%
STAIRS ($<$ 10)	56	64	67	67
STAIRS ($\geq$ 10)	50	47	50	50
STEP	64	69	69	67
STEPS (2–4)	56	61	61	61
GRADUAL SLOPES	78	75	64	67
STEEP SLOPES	56	69	75	72
OPEN/CLOSE DOORS	75	78	89	94
NONE OF THE ABOVE	8	3	–	3

Key
Total number of parents (n) = 36 $<$ = *less than*
Total number of young people (n) = 36 $\geq$ = *greater than or equal to*
NB *Most young people can negotiate more than one obstacle.*

the study 69% of young people said they could manage a step without assistance and 64% said they could manage gradual slopes. Thus, when some young people and their parents said subjects could move around indoors without assistance, they were referring to totally flat environments. However, there was some improvement between the first and final set of interviews which partially reflects the mobility skills training offered within the respective schools.

Of those young people who use wheelchairs, a substantial proportion were unable to make transfers without assistance (Table 8.7). Whilst it is recognised that some are not physically able to make independent transfers because of the nature of their impairments, others could learn to make more transfers independently if more time was made available within school hours for them to develop and practise these skills.

TABLE 8.7: MAKING TRANSFERS FROM WHEELCHAIRS

Percentage who can transfer without assistance

	Initial Interview		Final Interview	
Transfers	Young People %	Parents %	Young People %	Parents %
SHOWER	33	40	50	47
BATH	42	40	56	47
CAR	50	50	67	58
BED	54	60	67	63
TOILET	54	70	67	63
CHAIR	67	75	72	74
FLOOR	58	70	67	74
LIFT	29	15	22	11
HOIST	8	10	11	5
NONE OF THE ABOVE	33	25	22	16

NB *Most young people can make more than one transfer.*

Outdoor Mobility

Outdoor mobility skills are important because of the need to lessen social isolation (see page **85**) and the frustration of not being able to go out without an able-bodied assistant. Outdoor mobility requires a working knowledge of the outdoor environment and the necessary organisational skills to combine this with the ability to negotiate obstacles. Sixty-one per cent of young people and 47% of their parents said the subjects could move around outdoors without assistance, with or without aids. Once again, when questioned further about specific obstacles, although the percentages were lower (Table 8.8), there were improvements between the first and final sets of interviews reflecting participation in mobility skills training.

TABLE 8.8: NEGOTIATING OUTDOOR OBSTACLES

	Percentages of young people who negotiate obstacles without assistance			
	Initial Interview		Final Interview	
	Young People	Parents	Young People	Parents
Outdoor obstacles	%	%	%	%
UNEVEN SURFACES	74	57	82	74
KERBS	62	60	79	68
GRADUAL SLOPES	85	80	88	85
STEEP SLOPES	50	51	74	65
STEP	41	34	50	34
STEPS (2–10)	38	23	38	24
STEPS (10+)	21	11	24	15
CROSSING ROAD	47	40	53	41
PELICAN/ZEBRA CROSSINGS	53	49	56	59
LIFTS	53	46	53	47
ESCALATORS	24	17	26	29
OPENING/CLOSING DOORS	56	57	71	65
NONE OF THE ABOVE	6	9	9	9

NB *Most young people can negotiate more than one obstacle.*

Many schools use the RoSPA Mobility Awards as a tool when teaching people to become more independently mobile. Students are motivated to learn certain skills to the required standard, in order to qualify for their Bronze, Silver and Gold Awards. However, once an individual has achieved a gold award, she may think that she is as mobile as possible because she has reached the highest set standard. Many physiotherapists at schools visited were concerned about this, saying that individuals were less inclined to work at their mobility skills once they had obtained a gold award. Another difficulty is that since the tests for the awards generally take place in artificial environments eg. a simulated obstacle course, a successful candidate is not necessarily adept at performing the same skills in the "real" environment.

It is important not only to teach young people mobility skills, but also to give them the opportunity to use them both at school and at home. In school, mobility training should initially take place within a simulated environment, then in "real" situations with supervision. If students can demonstrate that they are aware of the hazards and can cope adequately, they should be allowed to go outside school premises unaccompanied. Some schools visited during this study shadowed the students before allowing them to go out totally alone ie. supervised students from a distance without their knowing they were being supervised. Although many parents interviewed said their children needed the skills to enable them to be independently mobile, many also said that they were reluctant to allow them to go out unaccompanied. If schools implemented the mobility training process outlined above and kept parents well informed of their child's progress, many of the fears would be alleviated. Some parents may also need additional support to enable them to allow their child to go out alone.

Although the development of outdoor mobility skills and the intervention with parents suggested above should take place on a long-term basis, short "independence" courses can supplement the training by teaching specific outdoor mobility skills. Many young people who learn these skills on short courses do retain them over time if they are given opportunities to practise them (Macredie and Bradshaw 1984). Thus, it is argued that more resources should be directed towards the development of these skills on short courses.

Maintaining and Storing Mobility Aids

Maintaining mobility aids involves very basic repairs, checking parts, recognising when they need fixing or replacing and knowing who to contact for maintenance and how to contact them. For example, young people who use wheelchairs provided by the Disablement Services Authority need to know how to check and inflate tyres, repair punctures, check brakes and seating, and check for any signs of wear and tear, and need also to know how to contact the local approved repairer service contracted out by the Disablement Services Authority.

Storing mobility aids is important in that it is necessary to store any spare equipment that is not in use and acquire the skills to do this either by directing a carer or by physically doing the task. Young people will need enough physical space to be able to do this. Those with only one piece of equipment eg. one wheelchair will not need to put it away for storage as they will need it even at night in case they want to get out of bed, but they will need to learn these skills to be able to put the wheelchair in a car.

Only 10% of those who used aids said that they could maintain them and only 14% could store them. There was no difference between the results from the first to the final set of interviews, suggesting that these skills were not covered during the two terms of the study in the participating schools. It is recommended that these skills are taught as an integral part of mobility skills training for those who use aids so that the aids do not become obstacles to other people and so that they are kept in good repair.

Transport

The most common modes of transport used by young people in this study are private cars (92%), school buses (83%) and taxis (15%). Although most young people used more than one form of transport, most forms encourage passivity, because users generally have no control over the vehicles and are picked up and taken home without needing to do anything actively. One special school visited during this study equipped all students with a map and asked them to direct the bus or taxi driver to their home. This is particularly important for those who are unable to use public transport. They can play a slightly more active role in their own transport by learning specific routes and the skills of directing someone. They may also acquire a stronger awareness of the roads and improve their sense of direction.

Fourteen per cent of young people interviewed said that they could use public transport independently, compared with 8% according to parents. Sixty-nine per cent of those interviewed reported not using public transport. The most common reason given for this was the inaccessibility of public transport (73%). However, other reasons were because they lacked practice (27%), or lacked confidence (20%), because of lack of opportunity to try (20%), because they did not know how to (12%), and because they were unable to handle money and thus pay the fares (12%).

Some of these barriers to using public transport can be overcome through appropriate training. Such training should include learning to use the rail networks, to read bus and train timetables, money management, and practise to build up confidence. Once again this training should take place within the real environment. All students should be aware of the services of TRIPSCOPE, a transport information telephone service which "seeks to simplify and expand people with disabilities transport options." Those who will not be physically able to use public transport unless it is made more accessible, should be taught the skills of organising alternative transport and have information about any local transport schemes such as Dial-a-Ride services and taxi-card schemes.

Once young people reach sixteen, they may have an assessment to see whether they could learn to drive. Mobility and driving assessments are carried out at Banstead Mobility Centre, the Mobility Advice and Vehicle Information Services and elsewhere. These assessments are available, for a fee, to all applicants. Those who can learn to drive should have access to information about adapted vehicles and the Motability scheme.

HOME MANAGEMENT

This section focuses on basic skills of home management: shopping and money management, kitchen skills, tidying, bedmaking, light cleaning and safety precautions. For most young people with disabilities, these skills should be taught with reference to moving into an independent living environment, and information about services available to facilitate independent living, including independent living schemes, should be made easily accessible. Arranging visits to adapted flats and inviting young adults with disabilities to speak, who are living independently both with and without personal care assistants, would be informative and encouraging. This would help in motivating students to learn the skills which, as every house keeper knows from personal experience, are essentially tedious.

Shopping and Money Management

The percentage of young people who had never been shopping decreased from 17% at the start to 6% by the end of the study. Of those who had been shopping in the month prior to each interview, 56% had been once or twice a week, 8% only once during the month. At initial interview, 36% of young people and 31% of their parents said that subjects could shop without any assistance. The difficulties outlined by young people covered a wide range, including carrying things around the shop (17%), travelling to shops unaccompanied (14%), reaching high shelves (11%), handling money (11%). The help which they said that they needed also covered a similar range, including help to get things from shelves (19%), someone to push their wheelchair (14%), supervision (11%), managing money (11%) and someone to carry things (8%). These results are promising in that the majority of young people who needed assistance were able to identify their difficulties and the help which they needed, although boys were less proficient at this than girls. This reflects the opportunities which parents and schools are giving young people to practise these skills.

Shopping skills, including the management of money must be taught within the real environment. As students get older, they should be taught the skills of budgeting within a limited income and be given opportunities to practise these skills when shopping. They should also be introduced to services offered ie., banks, building societies and post offices. Some schools visited during this study had a school bank on the premises to enable students to learn this aspect of money management. This is a High Street bank eg. Midland, which offers basic services and is run by older students with minimal supervision from staff.

In the Kitchen

At initial interview, 63% of young people said that they sometimes chose what they would like to eat for dinner or planned a meal at school, compared with 81% at final interview. The percentage of those who said that they could plan meals without any assistance rose from 39% to 61% at final interview, although those who needed assistance could not state their difficulties and indicate what help they required. These encouraging results, supported by evidence from school documents, show that schools participating in this study are teaching young people to plan meals. Problems remain with those young people who needed assistance, as they appeared to be unable to identify the type of assistance they needed. Would a group of similar-aged able-bodied young people be able to plan meals, and if not, would they know the sort of assistance which would be helpful? With this information, it might be possible to identify precise gaps in knowledge and to structure learning objectives to fill these gaps.

Students should be taught the skills of planning meals with both convenience foods and conventional foods. There is often a negative value judgement associated with convenience food, but as they exist, they should be used judiciously, if they are of good nutritional value. The researcher found all schools visited were teaching basic cookery skills, but fewer were teaching the skills of preparing convenience foods. It cannot be assumed that young people with disabilities will learn to prepare convenience foods without instruction, as many do not have opportunities to practise these skills in their home environment.

Table 8.9 indicates a slight improvement over time of the percentage of students who made hot drinks, snacks and simple meals. However, there were still 28% who said they had never been involved in doing these tasks at all. Whilst 50% reported being able to do these tasks without assistance, 22% said that they needed assistance. The difficulties outlined by those who needed assistance included inaccessible kitchens at home, lifting and pouring hot liquids, opening tins and general lack of confidence. Twelve per cent of parents said that they were too frightened to allow their child(ren) to use the kitchen (see page **156**).

TABLE 8.9: MAKING HOT DRINKS, SNACKS AND SIMPLE MEALS

	Percentage of Responses			
	Initial Interview		Final Interview	
	Young People	*Parents*	*Young People*	*Parents*
	%	%	%	%
HOT DRINKS	68	47	71	80
SNACKS	68	72	80	80
SIMPLE MEALS	38	36	54	60
NONE OF THE ABOVE	26	28	17	17

Despite the fears and possible hazards involved, young people should be taught the skills of making hot drinks, snacks and simple meals and be given opportunities to practise them at school. Both fears and hazards should be dealt with effectively to diminish both.

Having cooked a meal or snack, most students should be obliged to wash their dishes. Only 25% of young people reported that they washed dishes at least once a week. At initial interview, 56% of young people and 44% of parents said subjects could do this without assistance compared with 64% and 50% respectively at final interview. Interviews identified inaccessible sinks and lack of confidence as the major difficulties preventing subjects washing up.

It is important that some kitchen units should be accessible to those who use wheelchairs. For those that do not have accessible kitchens in their home environment, it is particularly important to identify both what they can achieve in a setting more suited to their needs and which adaptations prove useful to them. It would also be helpful if staff could find the time to conduct home visits, particularly to young people who use wheelchairs. The information gathered would help in teaching students skills which could then be used at home. Where home visits are not possible, schools could design a questionnaire for parents asking for basic information about their kitchen (Appendix 5).

In the Bedroom

75% of young people and 81% of parents said that subjects tidied their own area/room. Thirty-six per cent of interviewees reported that this was done at least once a week. At initial interview, 55% of young people and 61% of parents said subjects did not need any assistance, compared with the same percentage of young people and 72% of parents at final interview. The main difficulty identified was inability to reach things. However, few interviewees had disability equipment to help overcome this. Other difficulties experienced seem to relate more to adolescence than disability including lack of motivation, "can't please mum", "what's wrong with a messy room?".

61% of young people and 75% of parents said subjects made their own beds. At initial interview 50% of young people and 64% of parents said that subjects could do this without assistance compared with 58% and 64% respectively at final interview. The difficulties identified included handling sheets, lifting mattresses, tucking in sheets and changing duvet covers. Care of soiled linen and care of the mattress when the linen had been soiled was not mentioned by any of the young people with incontinence difficulties or their parents. This may be because young people knew what to do if their sheets became soiled or because they were too embarrassed to mention it, or it may not have occurred to them because someone else always dealt with it.

Light Cleaning

36% of young people had never done any light cleaning, namely dusting, polishing, hoovering, or sweeping the floor. Twenty-five per cent of young people and 19% of parents said that subjects could do light cleaning without assistance. The difficulties identified included handling heavy equipment, balancing and managing stairs. Would a group of similar-aged able-bodied young people be willing and able to clean, and identify the difficulties they would encounter in light cleaning? Since there is anecdotal evidence to suggest they would not, this aspect of a home-management skills programme is less important than those outlined in the previous sections.

Basic Repairs

Since boys and girls need the skills to do basic household repairs eg. putting on a plug and changing a light bulb, the majority of schools include these skills as part of the curriculum.

Safety

Young people with disabilities should be aware of basic safety measures. For example, carrying hot liquids presents a risk of scalding for everyone, especially young people with lower limb paralysis and those with tremors. They should be aware of this risk and be provided with an absorbent apron for protection when cooking, and also when taking hot drinks if they have difficulty drinking without spilling. However, the need to carry hot liquids can often be eliminated by attaching trolleys or tables to their wheelchairs. They should have access to any safety equipment which could lessen the chance of an accident at home such as safety guards on cookers. All young people should know the purpose of 999 services and how to use them in case of an emergency. However, basic household risks should be kept in proportion so as not to frighten a young person into avoiding any task which entails an element of risk.

LEISURE TIME

There are advantages in having a lot of leisure time if an individual has the skills, motivation and money to use it wisely. Ninety-seven per cent of the young people interviewed in this study said that watching television was one of their main hobbies. Other hobbies stated were listening to music (89%), reading (69%), and watching sport (42%). Although listening to music can be active, on the whole these hobbies facilitate passive rather than active involvement. Fewer young people said that they were involved in active hobbies which included collecting things (56%), playing sport (50%), playing a musical instrument (30%), and craftwork (22%). Since schools identify passivity as one of the main factors preventing young people with disabilities from becoming more independent (Table 3.1), students should be encouraged to engage in hobbies which demand more active involvement. However, effectively using leisure time does not always involve hobbies, for instance, entertaining friends and talking with music playing are valid ways of using time.

Going to clubs is one way of reducing social isolation and of actively using leisure time. 69% of young people said that they went to at least one club outside school hours (Table 8.10).

TABLE 8.10: INVOLVEMENT IN CLUBS

Percentage of Responses from Young People

	Initial Interview	Final Interview
	%	%
GUIDES	17	17
SCOUTS	14	14
PHAB	28	33
YOUTH CLUB	11	14
CHURCH	11	14
OTHER	19	33
NONE OF THE ABOVE	31	22

Also, more young people appear to attend segregated than integrated clubs: 41% compared with 28%. More of those who went to integrated clubs were from ordinary schools, and those with similar disabilities from special schools were more inclined to go to segregated clubs. Special schools acknowledge this anomaly and many are endeavouring to set up integrated leisure options.

As discussed in Chapter Six, ordinary and special schools should provide a broad range of accessible extra-curricular activities. The current range of extra-curricular activities offered by ordinary schools has been criticised, because research evidence has shown that it has a distinct sporting bias (Hendry and Marr 1985) and that the majority of activities are pursued only by a minority, mainly middle-class, academically able students (Hendry 1983). Thus, whilst it is argued that the range should include accessible sporting activities (see page **112**), other activities should also be offered. Adventure holidays which offer a wide range of activities could act as the initial motivating force for young people who appear uninterested in any leisure-time pursuits.

However, it should be remembered that students from all ability ranges tend to reject the types of activity promoted by ordinary schools in their own free time, ie. outside school hours and in their immediate post-school life (Hendry and Marr 1985). The reason given is that most schools' approaches to leisure are not based on the principles of empowerment. The predominating philosophy is one of "providing" leisure options rather than "enabling" individuals to choose and use leisure options (Mundy and Odum 1979).

There does not appear to be any comparable research conducted in special schools. However, the majority of special schools visited offered leisure opportunities in a similar way to ordinary schools by "providing" rather than "enabling". In one exception, the living skills team asked each student to choose a leisure activity and then worked out how to meet each individual's request – this was a tremendous administrative feat! Within the "enabling" approach, students need to survey and evaluate the leisure options available at school and in the wider community. In school, students with disabilities should be involved in designing the programme of extra-school activities which would include both ongoing and one-time only activities. In the community, young people will need to investigate how much activities would cost them and how transportation will be arranged.

Many of the skills necessary to choose and use leisure options are the same as for any other life choices eg. decision-making and relationship skills. Whilst young people should choose options they find fun and rewarding, they should also be encouraged to evaluate the age-appropriateness of the activity, and the opportunities that the activity offers for personal development, meeting others and expansion of leisure-time pursuits.

As a final comment, education for leisure could include planning for holidays within a limited income. In this way young people could learn the skills of evaluating the holidays on offer regarding their enjoyment potential, the factors outlined above, cost and accessibility.

SOLD TIME

Before looking at the skills of sold time and the results of this study, it is necessary to clarify some terms:

Sold time is defined as the time spent in open or sheltered employment, studying, training or doing voluntary work.

Work is defined as "any socially or personally useful or creative activity" (Hopson and Scally 1982).

A Career is defined as a lifestyle of choice.

A Student Profile is defined as "a systematic, comprehensive description and assessment of a pupil's academic and non-academic achievements, attributes and interests, set out in a format easy to interpret both by educational and non-educational users, and issued at the end of the student's period of secondary education". (AMMA 1983).

For all young people, their choice of career may or may not include paid employment, but it should include work. The options for those with disabilities are limited by the same variables as for able-bodied people – qualifications, experience, class, sex, race and sexual orientation plus any actual impairments which cannot be circumvented. They should have access to information about the options available to them when they leave school, and should be encouraged to explore what they want to do, without initial restrictions on what is deemed "reasonable" or probable. The more "realistic" choices can be left until the young person has confidence to accept what she can and cannot do. This would include information about paid employment, voluntary work, Open University courses, adult education centres, polytechnics, universities, and sheltered employment. Some information on quota schemes, equal opportunities and positive discrimination policies would also be helpful.

Gould (1986) has suggested that 14 years of age is a good time to start the process of transition from school to adult life for those with disabilities. When interviewing school leavers with disabilities, Hurst (1985) found that 58% thought that they did not receive enough help in learning about the world of employment. He found no significant difference between the views expressed by those in special and those in integrated schools. Whilst this is likely to be a reflection of the curricula offered in schools, it may be that students did not listen to this part of their education, because it was not immediately relevant to them. It is because of this and the culturally different experiences of many people with severe disabilities, that schools should ensure that students are aware of how to get access to specialist services when they need them eg. specialist careers officers, employment and education officers within the voluntary sector and disablement resettlement officers.

In one sense, the whole purpose of this book is to improve the career prospects for young people with disabilities. Thus, all the skills outlined in this book relate to sold time particularly "relating" skills and "information-seeking" skills eg. letter writing, visiting job centres and examining advertisements, and can enable some students to evaluate the options available, applicable and of interest to them. To some extent, this will depend on the type and severity of their impairments.

Students should be taught how to fill out application forms and the skills of attending interviews. Role-playing techniques with video feedback are particularly useful tools to teach interviewing skills in the same way as other relating skills (see page **93**). Some special and ordinary schools are also teaching the skills of entrepreneurship – groups of students aged 14 upwards are setting up small businesses within school to learn the basic skills of managing finances, etc. Some high street banks offer financial assistance to schools setting up these ventures.

Student profiles and the skills of learning from experience should help students to become more aware of their strengths and limitations, should give ideas about what to write on application forms, and should influence what they say in interviews. Students should be informed of the specific work skills needed in various types of sold time activities for instance strength, dexterity, stamina, co-ordination, writing and the more general skills eg. listening to and following instructions and punctuality. They should then be helped to match these skills with their individual abilities and potential.

The results of this study suggest that while the majority of young people would like paid employment to be part of their career, fewer expect to be employed when they leave school: Table 8.11 shows the preferences relating to post-school life, which young people aged 13 and above and their parents stated at initial and final interview, and Table 8.12 shows their expectations.

It has to be recognised that some young people with disabilities may not obtain full-time paid employment even if it is the lifestyle of their choice. This is partly because of society's attitudes towards people with disabilities which may result in deliberate or inadvertent discrimination. There are, therefore, strong arguments for suggesting that young people should also be taught about unemployment and the skills of coping with it. Students should be aware that unemployment is unlikely to disappear in the foreseeable future and will be experienced by many people, particularly those from minority groups. Hopson and Scally (1982) argue that schools should provide information about current causes and effects of unemployment, and unemployment trends. Awareness of attitudes to unemployment and their potential implications should also be raised. It is argued that this should be done both in a general sense and with respect to disability issues.

This section completes the broad areas described as working and playing. Having outlined the skills facets of the model, Part 3 of this book examines some practical issues involved in implementing the model in schools with young people with disabilities and involving their parents.

TABLE 8.11: POST-SCHOOL PREFERENCES

Number of Responses

Preferences	13–14 year olds Initial Interview		13–14 year olds Final Interview		15–16 year olds Initial Interview		15–16 year olds Final Interview	
	Young People	*Parents*	*Young People*	*Parents*	*Young People*	*Parents*	*Young People*	*Parents*
DON'T KNOW	4	3	4	7	1	3	1	–
WORK WITH CHILDREN	1	1	1	1	–	–	2	1
SECRETARY	–	1	–	–	1	–	1	–
NURSING	–	1	–	–	1	1	1	–
WORK IN A BANK	–	–	1	–	–	–	1	–
STUDY LAW	1	1	1	–	–	–	1	–
MECHANIC	1	1	1	1	–	–	1	–
COLLEGE	1	–	1	1	1	1	1	1
HAIRDRESSING	–	2	–	1	1	–	1	–
ARTIST	–	2	–	–	1	–	1	–
SING	2	1	2	1	1	–	1	–
LEARN TYPING	2	–	1	2	–	–	–	–
FISHERMAN	–	–	–	1	–	–	–	–
COMPUTER PROGRAMMER	3	3	3	2	–	–	–	1
CLOTHES DESIGNER	1	–	1	–	2	–	1	1
LEAVE HOME	1	–	1	1	1	1	–	1
WORK WITH DISABLED PEOPLE	–	2	–	–	–	1	–	1
WORK WITH ANIMALS	–	–	–	–	–	1	–	–
BEAUTICIAN	–	–	–	–	–	2	–	–
MODEL	–	–	1	1	–	–	–	–
OTHER	3	–	3	1	4	–	4	4

Key
Number of 13–14 year olds (n) = 16
Number of 15–16 year olds (n) = 9

TABLE 8.12: POST-SCHOOL EXPECTATIONS

Age of Subjects

Expectations	13–14 year olds				15–16 year olds			
	Initial Interview		Final Interview		Initial Interview		Final Interview	
	Young People	Parents	Young People	Parents	Young People	Parents	Young People	Parents
DON'T KNOW	4	10	7	7	2	2	1	3
LIVING WITH PARENTS	5	1	1	–	–	1	–	–
WORKING IN THE DAY	–	–	–	1	1	–	–	–
MAKING A RECORD	1	–	–	–	–	–	–	–
COLLEGE	1	1	1	1	1	1	2	2
SECRETARIAL WORK	–	1	1	1	3	1	–	–
ACCOUNTS WORK	1	–	–	–	–	–	–	–
TEACH	–	–	–	–	1	–	–	1
GO TO LEISURE CENTRE	1	–	–	–	–	–	–	–
CAR MAINTENANCE	–	–	–	–	1	–	–	–
LIVE IN THE COUNTRY	1	–	–	–	–	–	–	–
LIVE IN OWN HOME	–	–	–	–	1	1	–	–
DESIGNER	1	–	–	–	–	–	–	1
LEAVE HOME	–	–	–	–	–	1	–	1
NOT THOUGHT ABOUT IT	1	–	–	–	–	–	–	–
COMPUTING	–	1	1	3	–	–	–	1
CARE WORK	–	–	–	–	–	2	–	–
LEARN TO DRIVE	–	–	1	1	–	–	–	–
OTHER	–	–	–	2	–	–	–	3

Key
Number of 13–14 year olds (n) = 14
Number of 15–16 year olds (n) = 7

PART THREE

Implementing the Model

CHAPTER NINE
Practical Curriculum Issues

The Holographic Model of Living Skills offers a dynamic framework for helping young people with disabilities to become more self-empowered. It could be implemented as a cross-curriculum theme, or a separate course. The latter would be easier to co-ordinate. The effective implementation of this curriculum framework requires the allocation of considerable resources, especially time. It is recognised that the curriculum is crowded and teachers and other school staff already have many demands on them, but this does not diminish the special need for young people with disabilities to learn the physical, intellectual and emotional skills that empower them. Young people with disabilities also need the same academic preparation as their peers. The major objective is to balance academic preparation with education in the skills for living as outlined in this book. Is it more important for young people to achieve their maximum intellectually or should some of their academic training be neglected for training in living skills? Where does the compromise between the two occur? When the National Curriculum is implemented, the Statements of Special Educational Needs under the Education Act 1981 will direct the extent to which the National Curriculum requirements will be modified or disapplied completely for each student. However, this conflict will remain unresolved.

First, this chapter will consider the current attempts to cope with these conflicting demands. Secondly, it will consider some of the implications for staff support, training and resources. Finally, this chapter will look at some of the national issues involved in effective implementation of the Holographic Model of Living Skills.

ORDINARY SCHOOLS

The main issues involved in implementation of the Holographic Model of Living Skills in ordinary schools are:
- conflict between full integration and acknowledgement of disability issues
- overcrowded curriculum.

It is important to consider the philosophy behind the integration of young people with disabilities. There is currently a trend towards "absolute integration", whereby students with disabilities have exactly the same curriculum as their peers. However, many students with disabilities need explicit teaching of some skills that their peers learn automatically at an earlier age and need to learn some skills that their peers do not. It also takes many students with disabilities longer than their peers to conduct many maintenance time skills.

Whilst on the one hand, many students with disabilities want to be "treated" exactly the same as their peers, so conforming to normality, on the other hand it is important that students do not deny their disability in order to be accepted by their peers. Although it can be stigmatising for students with disabilities to be offered anything different in school, it is important that schools recognise and address the individual needs of students with disabilities so they learn to accept their disabilities rather than pretend they have none. Thus, it is appropriate to offer some separate group and/or individual work. But when?

Currently, the skills for living outlined in this book come under a number of different subjects, and the development of maintenance time skills is given no timetabled room at all. Some ordinary schools will not accept students with disabilities unless they are proficient at self-care skills. Of those that do address maintenance time skills, a number of different structures are used:
- use of short courses
- use of break-times
- withdrawal from physical education lessons
- withdrawal from personal and social education lessons
- an "option" subject for students aged 14 and above
- withdrawal from an academic subject
- use of home economics lessons.

Some ordinary schools send students on residential short courses, to develop maintenance time skills, offered by the voluntary sector, a few health authorities and social services departments. The courses are a useful "top-up" but they are not sufficient for the development and use of maintenance time skills on a long-term basis. The key to successful maintenance time skills development is covered in the home–school liaison section (see page **156**).

Break-times are sometimes used because whilst the school timetable fails to provide adequate time in any other part of the school day, individual staff recognise the importance of developing basic maintenance time skills. However, using break-times to help young people with disabilities develop these skills provides insufficient time for staff to work on the skills effectively and systematically. Moreover, it means that students miss out on one of the few opportunities to mix with their peers, and this exacerbates the problems many experience with respect to social isolation and developing and maintaining relationships. Everyone needs some free time during the day: there is great value for students in learning how to use this time, so it is counter-productive to structure their only guaranteed discretionary time with peers.

It is also inappropriate to withdraw students from physical education lessons which offer opportunities for social interaction and much needed exercise. Changing for physical education may be an appropriate time to work on some sub-skills of dressing and undressing, but this should not take up the whole period. It is better to work on one skill at a time and to give assistance for the remaining skills to ensure that students are not excluded from physical activities and that other students are not neglected. It is important that these skills are developed in relation to individual programmes so that progress can be monitored.

Personal and social education lessons should help young people to take more control over their own lives.

Personal and social education is the ideal forum for exploring the skills for living relevant to all young people and the general issues around disability and handicap. Topics that could and sometimes are already included are:

- disability and handicap
- prejudice
- alternative forms of communication
- aids and adaptations
- roles of various paramedical staff
- media imagery.

Withdrawal from these lessons to develop maintenance time skills at the expense of developing other crucial living skills is counter-productive.

In some ordinary schools, many students with disabilities are encouraged to take a "living skills" option in their fourth and fifth year at school, rather than take another academic subject. Although these courses are valuable, as argued before, students should be taught these skills at an earlier age, ie. before they are 14 years old.

Finally, some maintenance time skills are successfully developed through the Home Economics curriculum, namely eating and drinking for healthy living and home-management skills.

It is important to ensure that any lessons/sessions predominantly geared to able-bodied students are perceived by disabled students as relevant to them. There are two complementary ways of doing this:
- Support teaching
- Segregated group work.

Support teaching enables one staff member to concern herself with the individual needs and abilities within the group, whilst the other conducts the group. Maintenance time skills are effectively developed if a support teaching system is used, so that students with disabilities have their needs met but not at the expense of other students in the class. Some of the sensitive issues arising from mainstream sessions can also be dealt with appropriately within a support teaching system. Alternatively, the staff may decide to refer an individual to the school's counsellor (if there is one), or to talk to the student individually after the mainstream session. It may be appropriate to ask the student to raise the issue in a segregated group of students with disabilities.

There also seems to be a need for timetabled, segregated group work with young people with disabilities within ordinary schools which addresses issues particularly pertinent to them. This will be easier to arrange in schools with a number of students with disabilities. When there are only one or two, students from different schools within the borough could meet together in one of the schools, although this would be costly and time-consuming to arrange in large and rural areas. Groups should be conducted by two facilitators from inside and outside the school, preferably at least one of whom has a disability. Since it is important to move away from connections between impairments and illness, at least one of the facilitators should be a non-medical professional. It is best if topics are suggested by the students themselves, but it is useful to try to include the following types of issues:
- the disabling effects of given impairments
- society's attitudes to disability and handicap
- stigma
- sexuality and disability
- aids and adaptations
- allowances and benefits
- community resources for people with disabilities
- the self-advocacy movement
- social isolation
- over-protection
- body image
- issues that have arisen in the mainstream personal and social education lessons with their specific implications for students with disabilities.

The skills for living outlined in this book must be developed through a structured, systematic programme sufficiently flexible to meet individual needs. It must be acknowledged that there is not a way of offering systematic, effective education in all living skills without substituting this for some other part of the school curriculum. Academic subjects appear to be more highly valued than non-academic ones as students are rarely withdrawn from the former. But the increasing number of Personal and Social Education courses indicates that there is a growing belief that non-academic education is of equal value to academic education in the preparation for adult life. Withdrawal from an academic subject rather than a non-academic subject may be appropriate for some students with disabilities. It may be helpful if this occurred earlier than the fourth year. Students and their parents should choose together which subject to drop. This not only applies to developing maintenance time skills but also may apply to other skills of particular concern to students with disabilities.

The next section explores some of the issues of implementation in special schools. However, since there is considerable overlap between implementation in ordinary and special schools, many of the issues already outlined are equally applicable to special schools and will not be repeated in the next section.

SPECIAL SCHOOLS

In essence, there are three main issues particularly pertinent to special schools:

- the involvement of the full interdisciplinary team
- structuring personal and social education
- the development and adaptation of materials geared to an intellectually and physically disabled population.

In general, it is recognised that young people educated in special schools need considerable contact with able-bodied young people if they are to become more independent in their adult lives.

Developing maintenance time skills is increasingly part of special school curricula but continues to be seen primarily as the role of paramedical professionals and non-teaching assistants. It is essential that there is sufficient negotiation and communication between all staff, so that structured living skills programmes can be developed by the full interdisciplinary team. Within residential schools, the role of the care staff should be given particular consideration.

Since the implementation of the Education Act 1981, many special schools are educating students who are less intellectually able than those of a decade ago. This has led to a considerable change in practice, including the methods of teaching and the complexity and specificity of the measurement tools used. However, the broad aim of self-empowerment is the same for those at all levels of ability. Part of personal and social education is seen by some as teaching young people to conform to social norms and conventions. This is in sharp contrast to the aims of personal and social education advocated in this book, which is to enable young people to take more control over their lives. When interviewing staff within special schools, working towards independence was seen by the majority to underpin the whole school education. However, the ways that this was to be achieved were much more vague. Very few of the schools timetabled Personal and Social Education which seemed to leave the development of many skills (eg. decision making, managing conflict, coping with loss and grief and time management) to chance. While special schools seemed to give the most credence to the value of Personal and Social Education, they also did less to clarify what this entailed.

Implementing structured Personal and Social Education curricula is essential. However, many of the materials designed to help staff develop and implement these curricula are geared towards an intellectually able population. Adapting these materials needs both time and an in-depth understanding of the principles of active learning. In the long term, research into the best ways of adapting these materials is needed, but in the meantime, interdisciplinary staff teams need to adapt some of the existing materials to meet the needs of their specific populations (see Appendix 7).

Having raised these issues, the next section will look at the basic elements of introducing a living skills curriculum within all schools.

INTRODUCING AND EVALUATING A SKILLS FOR LIVING CURRICULUM

The research indicates that schools which have a clear working policy document on enabling students to become more independent are more likely to meet this overall aim. Such policies specify clear aims and need sufficient flexibility to consider the individual needs of each student. The documents need to state the aims of the school in relation to developing independence amongst its students, and the assessment, planning and evaluation procedures required to put the aims into practice, eg. staff training and staff support. Since Local Education Authorities play a significant role within maintained schools, their guidance is essential.

The leadership and support of the head teacher is crucial to the success of the living skills curriculum within any type of school. She must understand and be committed to the aims and objectives of the work, and provide adequate support for staff in designing and implementing the curriculum. Every staff member within the school needs to be aware of and committed to the aims and objectives of the curriculum, because each will indirectly or directly be involved with the development of these skills. However, recruitment of staff to be involved actively and directly in implementing this curriculum should be on a voluntary basis. The broader the skills and abilities of the staff team, the broader the living skills course offered.

It is also important to evaluate the living skills curriculum with a systematic review. This enables the staff team to assess the aspects of the curriculum that are successful and those that need to be improved and it enables individual staff to explore the effectiveness of a variety of different assessment and teaching methods. Time needs to be allocated within the school day for the relevant staff members to come together to plan and discuss the curriculum, ie. to form a curriculum study group. Given inevitable time constraints, different aspects of the programmes offered will be considered at different times. Where it is not possible to set time aside to discuss living skills specifically, it is important to ensure systematically that all aspects of a living skills curriculum are addressed within at least one subject area. However, this raises the fear that living skills will be overlooked. Ideally, evaluation of a living skills curriculum should be conducted on a long-term basis, requiring follow-up studies with ex-students to determine the impact on post-school lives.

The next section discusses co-ordination of individual living skills programmes.

CO-ORDINATION

The importance of efficient communication systems between disciplines is well documented in the literature (Foster *et al.* 1977). Efficient communication helps develop consistency so that students receive clear messages from the whole staff team. Regular staff meetings can provide a forum for accurate exchange of information, if there is a fundamental commitment from all team members to clear communication. It is essential that individuals from each discipline make active attempts to translate their professional jargon for each other to overcome the barriers to interdisciplinary work. Whilst it is important to pass on most information, there may be some confidential information given to an individual staff member, (eg. a counsellor) that it is unnecessary for the whole staff team to know. However, it is important that the individual staff member concerned can discuss this information with her supervisor: total confidentiality may not be possible and staff need to be aware of their limitations. This raises the issue of confidentiality which could be explored within staff meetings.

Given the sheer number of staff frequently involved with young people with disabilities, a member of the team should undertake the role of co-ordinator

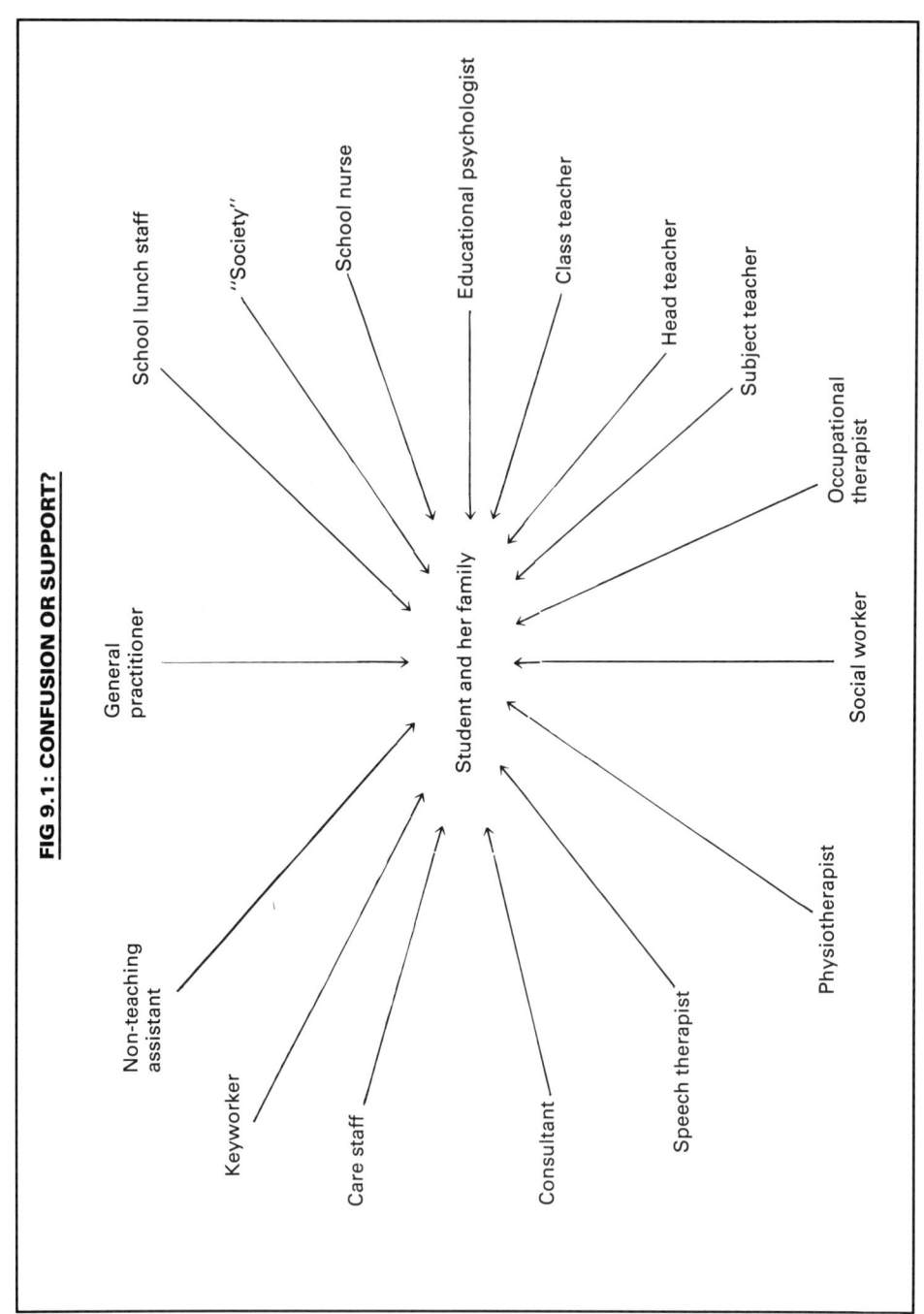

for each student, so acting as the link person. This is very important, otherwise it is the student and her family who are left in the middle to make sense of it all (see Fig 9.1).

The co-ordinator's role would be to ensure that living skills are covered systematically, so that as much as possible each student and her family's needs are met and so that they receive consistent guidance from everyone. This would be a two-way process in that the co-ordinator would also help to meet the needs of the staff team, by gathering information from the family and from individual team members. The role would involve considerable contact with the whole family, arranging meetings and drawing together advice and assessments from all team members. If it is accepted that enabling young people to become more independent is about empowerment, the most appropriate co-ordinator is the person that the young person and her family feels most comfortable with, and most able to trust. It is therefore impossible to designate any one profession. Since this role will be time-consuming, it is essential that the staff member with this role is allocated sufficient time within the school day to conduct all the necessary tasks. At the same time, she must be able to command credibility within the staff as a whole. By linking staff in this way, everyone's work is made easier as no one is working in isolation or ignorance.

If all the information gathered is stored on a computer data base, specific information can be generated easily and so is more accessible. This may reduce the number of hours needed to fulfil adequately the co-ordinator's role. The co-ordinator will be most effective if there are clear assessment, planning and evaluation procedures. These will be discussed in the next chapter.

PROFILING: ASSESSMENT, PLANNING AND EVALUATING

Whilst the overall aim of self-empowerment is the same for all students, the specific objectives for each student differ at any given time. As stated before, it is essential to assess each individual, to identify priorities, state objectives and evaluate whether these have been achieved with each student. Priorities will change continually as the student's desires and needs change. Since a profiling system gives sufficient emphasis to self-assessment, planning and evaluation, it is a useful tool in helping young people with disabilities to become more independent.

Involving students in their own assessment procedures requires a considerable amount of time. With profiling, assessment could no longer be seen as something extra above and beyond normal duties. It requires a change in current practice for many staff. This has inevitable consequences for training: basic counselling skills, the skills of giving and receiving feedback and negotiation are likely to enable staff to develop the open and trusting relationships needed if the full value of profiling is to be achieved (Pearce 1982). Profiling could provide the opportunity for assessment to become part of the curriculum when staff are given adequate time and training to use the tool effectively: the tool can only be as effective as those responsible for its implementation.

The initial assessment should establish the extent of known communicated information upon which a systematic approach can be based. The assessment should examine knowledge, attitudes and skills. This information may be gained from a number of different sources:

- students themselves
- parents
- Statements made under Section 7 of the Education Act 1981
- feeder schools
- care staff
- medical professionals
- paramedical professionals
- teachers
- social workers (if involved)
- observation of students in a variety of settings, including a residential setting, therapy sessions, in the community, in break-times and in formal and informal lessons
- voluntary agencies.

Each facet of the Holographic Model needs some form of assessment, but the format for each may be significantly different. There are a number of published assessment charts which cover maintenance time skills, such as Mossford Assessment Chart, Copewell Curriculum (see page **179**). These checklists are primarily designed within a behavioural philosophy, ie. if an individual can be taught to change her behaviour, the other facets of independence will automatically follow. Each skill area is divided into a number of sub-skills, so that students and staff can pinpoint the exact area of difficulty in the development of any particular skill. Whilst these checklists are useful for the development of some maintenance time skills, they are far less useful in the development of attitudes and other living skills, for instance skills of developing the self, and learning. Further research is needed into assessment of attitudes and these other living skills.

Overall, assessment should be criterion-referenced rather than norm-referenced. This will have to be taught to individual students who may tend to compare themselves to others. It is more effective to examine an individual's own level of development in certain tasks and attitudes rather than comparing an individual's performance with others in the group (Hutchinson and Tennyson 1986). As stated before, the initial assessment should be the starting point of the planning and evaluation process rather than an end-point in itself. After the initial assessment, the whole team should establish priorities and plan the individual programme in Individual Programme Planning (IPP) meetings with the co-ordinator collating all of the recommendations (see page **139**). As in some special schools, IPP meetings should be every half-term if possible, or at the least termly. In these meetings, the team should identify long-term and short-term objectives and immediate priorities. It is possible to evaluate intervention only if the aims of the intervention are clear. Some aspects of the living skills curriculum will be pre-planned, so it is essential that those aspects of the programme that are non-negotiable are stated explicitly at the IPP meetings. It is recommended that all students, aged 11 and upwards, should participate in these meetings so that they can begin to gain more control of their lives and the support they receive. If this is unrealistic or deemed inappropriate according to school policy, one suitable member of staff should ensure that the students' views are put forward at the meeting so that someone is playing their role. The views of students and their parents should be considered with utmost gravity because first, staff are trying to meet their needs and secondly, because the student and parents are most likely to work hardest at goals they have chosen.

As with assessment procedures, the planning procedures evaluated in the current study were based mainly on the principles of behaviourism. Planning was based on task-analysis, ie. broad goals were reduced to smaller goals. In its purest form, this approach does not take account of factors such as self-image, motivation and confidence. Objectives set during IPP meetings should be divided into three areas:
- attitudes
- knowledge
- skills.

Having identified objectives within IPP meetings, contracting can be a useful tool for successful programme implementation. Each team member writes down her role in the implementation of goals set and all those involved sign and receive a copy of the collated document. Contracting enables students to take more responsibility for their own learning. Contracting can take place either in IPP meetings, or on an individual basis beween co-ordinator and student. Once individual goals are identified, it is necessary to monitor and evaluate the implementation of these goals. As has already become clear, effective monitoring of individual programmes is possible only if the formative assessment and planning procedures have been followed through.

Individualised evaluation procedures are crucial to the success of education towards self-empowerment and independence, and so are too important to be left to staff to do in their spare time. It is essential that they are seen as part of the curriculum and are allocated sufficient time within the school day. The visits conducted in this study showed that staff were expected in their spare time to monitor students' progress. As a result, some of the documents were either inadequately filled in or not filled in at all. Although it is recognised that schools are under heavy pressure from all sides, this incomplete documentation leads to vague pictures of students' development, and can result in poor quality information exchange between team members.

The student herself should be seen as the key person in her evaluation. Self-assessment can be written or oral; it can take the form of diaries, assignments, discussion, participation and talks. It is in itself an invaluable skill in becoming more self-empowered. Furthermore, it is an excellent opportunity to improve dialogues between students and staff. However, it is important to recognise that students may be inclined to state views about themselves that they believe staff want to hear. The following example of one girl's contribution to her Individual Programme Plan (IPP) report illustrates the potential pitfall of self-assessment:

> "*My Feelings about my IPP Report*
>
> I could do an awful lot better in all the areas, especially in the independence area and hobbies area.
>
> I could do better in group discussion and not be so self-centred.
>
> I could also do more to motivate myself.
>
> I could also do a lot more to control my moods.
>
> I would like to prove to everyone especially Audrey and Mum and Dad that I can be trusted and more independent.
>
> I am worried about leaving because I'm thinking 'Oh help, what am I going to do after College?' I haven't really worried about it until recently. Now it's just dawned on me that I've only got another year.
>
> *Medication*
>
> I was stopped self admin because they found tablet bottles in my drawer. I don't know why I did! I think I was scared to tell anyone that I had accidently forgotten to take them. Looking back on it I wish I had told them.
>
> *Mobility*
>
> I think at last I have finally accepted that I'm going to be in a wheelchair for the rest of my life and I hate relying on my chair to get me places. I only wish I could walk again. I also want to be able to drive a car in the near future."

To overcome this, each student should be encouraged to say exactly what she thinks, rather than to merely confirm staff opinions. Her overall self-assessment, including the ways she thinks she has changed and improved should be discussed with her individual programme co-ordinator with reference to any agreed contract. The co-ordinator could represent the views of the staff, or just state her own views and leave other staff to state their views at the IPP meeting. The IPP meetings can be used to evaluate the student's development with respect to the objectives and/or the contract. This would enable parents to be actively involved in the process. Given that individual objectives are sub-divided into knowledge, attitudes and skills, so should the evaluation of individual's progress.

The effective implementation of a living skills curriculum is complex, and there are a number of implications for staff support, staff training and resources which must be addressed. The following sections consider each implication.

STAFF SUPPORT

"There is a need for the pastoral care of staff to be recognised as a field in its own right, requiring the development of an approach and expertise, complementary to that made available to pupils." (Lawley 1985)

The proposals for empowerment outlined in this book require considerable re-evaluation of current practice and this is stressful for those who have become accustomed to working in a particular way. It is essential that staff feel empowered rather than victimised by yet another progressive idea so that they can actively enable young people with disabilities to become more independent.

The notion of pastoral care for students is now generally accepted, and acted upon to varying degrees according to the belief systems underlying individual schools. However, the notion of pastoral care for staff is rarely considered in practice although it has received some attention in the literature (Dunham 1987). This may reflect a strong coping ethic within the professions, whereby needing support is misguidedly equated with failure and an inability to cope.

While staff generally support each other informally in break-times, there should also be formal support systems within schools as exist within other agencies, eg. social services. Support can be offered in "staff support groups" and in individual supervision sessions. "Staff support groups" are usually held weekly when all members of staff (or staff for one year group in large schools) meet to discuss issues that concern any individual team members. The groups are not planning meetings for individual students or general policy meetings: the focus is on support and working through problems and difficulties arising at work.

Supervision is concerned with active listening and is a forum for the supervised individual to explore in a safe situation issues directly or indirectly connected with her work. Middle-management within schools usually combine the roles of supervisor and line manager, which may cause them some conflict. It is crucial that middle-management staff also have supervision as, without this support, they will be unable to facilitate development in their team members, as they themselves are stressed (Dunham 1984). However, local education authorities rarely provide resources for this kind of supervision. It might be helpful to employ outside supervisors who do not also hold power as line managers. It is equally important that staff conducting groups on sensitive issues have skilled supervision.

Care staff and non-teaching assistants often have less credibility within the staff hierarchy than other professionals. Because of this and a lack of training, some may feel intimidated by other professionals at meetings about students. This may mean that some valuable input is lost. Staff support groups and regular supervision offer opportunities for them to air their feelings, so possibly enabling them to become more vocal. Support groups also encourage other professionals to recognise the difficulties faced by care staff and to value their contribution as part of the interdisciplinary team.

STAFF TRAINING

The results of this study suggest that some professionals receive no in-service training to familiarise themselves with the self-care needs of young people with disabilities (see Table 9.1).

TABLE 9.1: IN-SERVICE TRAINING

	Ordinary Schools		Special Schools	
	With Unit	Full Integration	Residential	Day
Training	4	6	17	11
No Training	4	9	4	14

Number of Schools (n) = 69

Table 9.2 shows a breakdown of school staff who receive in-service training. It should be noted that auxiliary staff were rarely included in the training offered. This may lead to confusion and undermining of objectives set by other staff members.

It is important that all school staff receive in-service training, especially non-teaching assistants and care staff who often have no previous professional

TABLE 9.2: SCHOOL STAFF THAT RECEIVE TRAINING

	Ordinary School	Special School
TEACHERS	5	24
CARE STAFF (RESIDENTIAL)	–	18
NURSING STAFF	3	18
NON-TEACHING ASSISTANTS	6	19
AUXILIARY STAFF	–	2
SPECIAL NEEDS CO-ORDINATOR	3	–
PARAMEDICS	3	18

Number of Schools (n) = 38

training. In-service training could be covered under the auspices of the broader term – staff development workshops. Figure 9.2 offers some suggestions for staff development workshops that relate to implementing the Holographic Model of Living Skills. The suggestions are geared towards non-teaching assistants and care staff, although other professionals may find some of them useful. Some generic in-service training may lead to better communication between disciplines. A good deal of the training could be

---

FIG 9.2: SUGGESTIONS FOR STAFF DEVELOPMENT WORKSHOPS

1. Disability Awareness courses including different models of disability.
2. Disability Issues in Education, including causes and implications of the most common types of impairment.
3. Community Care: understanding other agencies' roles including social services, area health authorities, voluntary agencies and the careers service.
4. Staff roles within the school.
5. Use of Individual Programme Plans and Profiling.
6. Lifting techniques.
7. Working with young people with progressive conditions.
8. Sexuality and Disability.
9. Counselling Skills.
10. Group Work Skills.
11. Stress Management and Managing Change.
12. The Skills of Developing Self.
13. The Skills of Learning.
14. The Skills of Relating.
15. The Skills of Working and Playing.
16. Staff Value Clarification Exercises.

offered by staff within the school who have the appropriate skills. For example, sessions on group work skills could be conducted by occupational therapists who may have learnt about group dynamics within their professional training. Other training may need to be provided by outsiders, eg. training on sexuality and disability.

RESOURCES

The main resources needed to implement the Holographic Model of Living Skills are:

- time
- appropriate interdisciplinary staffing including school counsellors and occupational therapists, and professionals of all disciplines with disabilities
- active support from social services and the careers service
- support teams of people with disabilities
- 24-hour resource
- shared resources between special and ordinary schools
- empowering physical environment.

This section expands upon the nature of these resources.

A fundamental sparse resource is time! There needs to be sufficient time allocated within the curriculum for students to develop living skills, and sufficient time allocated within the school day to document and administer the procedures outlined in this chapter.

There is also a need for adequate and appropriate staffing. Within ordinary schools there appears to be a shortage of paramedical support, particularly occupational therapists. Occupational therapists not only provide expertise in maintenance time skills development but also have group work skills training. Within both ordinary and special schools there appears to be a shortage of counsellors and professionals with disabilities of any discipline. There is also anecdotal evidence to suggest that many schools have inadequate support from social services and the careers service.

There is also a need for professionals with group work skills to conduct groups exploring many of the issues raised in this book. These could be occupational therapists as indicated above, or educational psychologists, group-work counsellors, or teachers with appropriate training. It is essential that staff conducting these groups have supervision from experienced group therapists.

As has become apparent, the effective implementation of the Holographic Model of Living Skills requires a full interdisciplinary team. Although the national shortage of occupational therapists is recognised, the shortage of school counsellors does not appear to have received due attention. The need for counselling is emphasised in some pastoral care literature (eg. Lowe 1988) and is reflected in the anecdotal evidence that suggests many school staff find themselves acting in a counselling role as there is no qualified person to whom to turn. We make no apologies for re-emphasising that "amateur" counsellors (ie. those that are untrained or inadequately trained) can be counter-productive.

A counsellor is defined as "someone who has been trained for some form of counselling that is to help another to deal with personal difficulties, to resolve problems of behaviour or choice and to make use of personal resources" (Blackham 1978).

The British Association for Counselling defines counselling in the following way: "people become engaged in counselling when a person, occupying regularly or temporarily the role of counsellor offers or agrees explicitly to offer time, attention and respect to another person or persons temporarily in the role of client. The task of counselling is to give the client an opportunity to explore, discover and clarify ways of living more resourcefully and towards a greater well-being." It is essential that those potentially in the role of counsellor who cannot offer time to a particular student, state that clearly so that they do not give false expectations.

It is helpful if counsellors have, at some point, been in the client role. Those counselling young people with disabilities must be aware of disability issues. Counselling can enable individuals to take full advantage of all the facilities available to them. It is essentially a process of learning about self, of growth and development which often involves exploring negative self-image and general concerns. Thus, access to counselling services is essential for many young people if they are to become more self-empowered.

The shortage of professionals with disabilities is another cause for grave concern. Relevant bodies need to examine recruiting procedures so that more people with disabilities are employed in special and ordinary schools. Some local education authorities have formed support teams of people with disabilities. These support teams can provide invaluable expert input into planning and implementation of living skills curricula.

Day schools, both ordinary and special, need access to a 24-hour adapted residential resource if they are to help young people learn to develop maintenance time skills. These flats are particularly useful for developing self-care skills, health-management and home-management skills. For this reason, many special schools have begun to build "independence" flats where students can learn and practise maintenance time skills with minimal assistance and/or by directing a carer. By staying in a residential setting without parents, students can build their self-confidence and learn to assess what they can and cannot do for themselves.

Ordinary schools integrating young people with disabilities should be using the resources of special schools and vice-versa, as recommended in the Warnock Report, 1978. For example, ordinary schools may be able to draw on the expertise in special schools and the 24-hour facilities in all residential and some day schools. Special schools may be able to draw on the different expertise in ordinary schools in terms of the wider curricula offered by sex education and personal and social education teachers.

Finally, it is important to examine the messages given to young people through the physical environment of the school: is any part of the school inaccessible to young people who use wheelchairs? Does any part of the environment infantilise young people with disabilities? For example, when visiting both ordinary and special schools, the researcher found that the accessible toilets often had curtains rather than doors. Since this structure is most commonly used for nursery school-aged children, it infantilises young people with disabilities and is therefore depowering. Recognising the inadequacy of facilities is the first step: attempts can then be made to remedy these deficiencies. Structural adaptations need not be very costly and with commitment from senior staff in the school, the local education authority can and should be pressed very hard (if necessary) to provide what is needed.

Having outlined the main resources needed to implement a living skills curriculum, it may be helpful to emphasise the probable long-term benefits in financial terms, although this cost-benefit argument is secondary. If students have access to these resources whilst at school, they are likely to need less support to live independently when they leave school so putting less strain on state financial resources.

NATIONAL ISSUES

Having discussed the main issues involved in the implementation of the Holographic Model of Living Skills in the short term, this section will consider some of the main national strategies that could help in the long-term implementation of the model. To investigate these issues and strategies effectively, there is a need for a National Advisory Council on Special Educational Needs. This could have a number of sub-committees to look at more specific aspects of education of young people with special needs, eg. a sub-group exploring living skills and the national curriculum and a sub-group investigating training needs.

The sub-group exploring living skills and the national curriculum could, first and foremost, produce guidelines on designing and implementing a practical policy in relation to developing independence among young people with disabilities. This central initiative would help individual local education authorities and individual schools to develop their own policies with respect to their specific populations.

To make more time to teach living skills, the school day could be lengthened, school holidays could be shortened or the holiday allocation could be changed and a four-term year introduced. However, it could be argued that these suggestions put unfair extra pressure on young people with disabilities and their teachers. Therefore, it might be more appropriate to endeavour to change the educational rights of young people with disabilities so that they have the right to further education. This suggestion raises issues of the role of further education. Would it be a time to focus on living skills or on academic skills or both? As has already become apparent, we would argue that living skills should be taught from an early age, and not left until late adolescence.

By 1992, there will be no teacher training in special needs education as all teacher training will be generic. Whilst hopefully this will have advantages relating to how young people with disabilities will be perceived, there will also probably be shortcomings in generic training. Arguably, there is a need for a totally new training initiative, which looks at disability issues in education. To promote interdisciplinary work there should be a number of joint training initiatives among professional disciplines.

Non-teaching assistants and care staff often receive little formal training for their posts. Whilst some local education authorities are starting basic in-service training, it is argued that there should be a recognised standardised national training initiative for these essential staff members. At the moment, on the whole, the quality of work reflects the pay structure and lack of training and vice-versa, so this suggestion has implications for the pay awarded to non-teaching assistants and care staff. The idea of a national training initiative also gives rise to a number of questions, such as who would fund such training? Who should provide it? Who should set the national standards? What should be the role of the National Nursery Examination Board (NNEB)?

Furthermore, it is important that non-teaching assistants are assured of their job, if they are no longer needed by the student to whom they were assigned initially. In some local education authorities, those non-teaching assistants who successfully encourage students to be more independent are working their way out of employment, and those who inadvertently encourage dependence have secured employment. This somewhat absurd situation has been rectified by some local education authorities who employ a pool of non-teaching assistants, rather than employing a particular non-teaching assistant for a particular student. This strategy should be adopted nationally.

The advocated National Advisory Council on Special Educational Needs could address these issues and make recommendations on them.

SUMMARY

This chapter has looked at the main aspects of and issues involved in the implementation of the Holographic Model of Living Skills namely:

- issues pertinent to ordinary schools
- issues pertinent to special schools
- introducing and evaluating a living skills curriculum
- co-ordination of living skills programmes
- profiling, assessment, planning and evaluation
- staff support
- staff training
- resources
- national issues.

As a final comment, it is important to recognise that this book can only raise issues and make suggestions. It is in the nature of this book that these cannot be expanded upon as almost every section could be a book in its own right!

CHAPTER TEN
Parents

This chapter examines some of the issues involved in working with parents in implementing the Holographic Model of Living Skills, and is based on the assumption of parents as partners in education. It attempts to address the questions of the home–school relationship implied by partnership. It is helpful first to consider some of the underlying processes behind home–school interaction and then make recommendations for practical strategies of liaison.

Parents should be partners in the education of their children. Whilst most would accept this statement in theory, there are many reasons why it does not always happen in practice. At the risk of over-generalising, these reasons include:

- Parental indifference
- Parental dependency on child (see page **86**)
- Mutual suspicion between professionals and parents
- Stereotyping by professionals of parents – parents are seen as all-knowing or knowing nothing
- Conflicting perceptions of "reality" by parents and professionals
- Lack of access to information for parents
- Difficulties faced by parents on a day-to-day basis: parental anxiety about being a "good" parent
- Ethnic minority issues
- Lack of training for parents to become effective partners
- Inadequate support of parents.

THE BLAME GAME: HOME–SCHOOL RELATIONS

Mutual suspicion and stereotyping between parents and professionals undoubtedly is the major contributor to poor home–school liaison. The results of the postal questionnaires sent to schools (Table 3.1) show that parental attitudes were seen by many schools as one of the principal inhibiting factors to independence in terms of self-care: parental concern was the factor put down more often than any other. Then, when asked the extent of parental involvement and ways in which it was encouraged, the majority of replies seemed vague. For example, many respondents wrote "encouraged through home–school liaison"; "open-door policy" or "through annual case conferences".

In the course of visits to schools it was noted that staff attitudes to parents seemed largely to fall into two main categories: either parents were perceived as knowing best, or they were assumed to be neurotic and over-protective. These two sets of reactions can be restated as two extremes of a continuum.

Parents know best ⟵—————————⟶ Parents know nothing

Schools' attempts to improve home–school relations through support groups and training days were often poorly attended. Research has shown that parental attitudes to teachers are no less prejudiced than teachers' attitudes to parents (Szwed 1986). Macbeth (1984) has described some of the processes involved in school–family relations as the "Blame Game" (Fig 10.1).

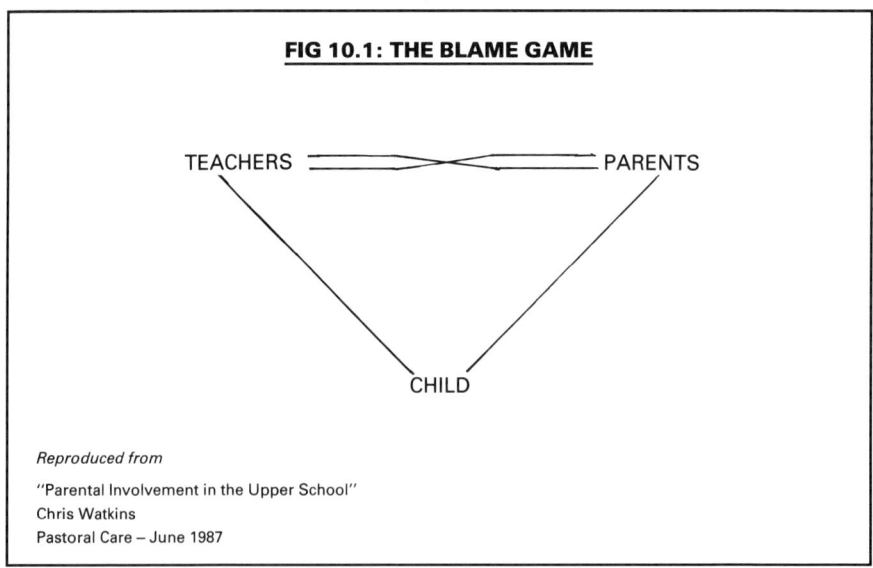

FIG 10.1: THE BLAME GAME

Reproduced from
"Parental Involvement in the Upper School"
Chris Watkins
Pastoral Care – June 1987

Parents and teachers are not communicating with each other effectively: the child is left to make sense of the situation, acting out different parts of herself in the two different environments. It is easy to see the similarities between this triangular system and the dynamics often inherent in the family. The teachers and parents are, in some ways, competing over the child and the child is left carrying the strain of the conflict (Watkins 1987). There is also the danger that some children will exploit this conflict, playing teachers off against parents and vice-versa; this possibility cannot be ignored.

The role of the teacher in this system is equally applicable to non-teaching assistants, care staff within residential settings, school nurses and the paramedical professionals. The "Blame Game" was applied to an ordinary setting, but given the familial atmosphere prevalent in many special schools, these processes are just as applicable in these environments.

Some parents may have differing perceptions of the "reality" of their child's situation than do the professionals working with the child. There can be many reasons for this: some parents may experience difficulties accepting their child has a disability and so might hold expectations for their child that professionals believe to be unrealistic, or parents' high expectations for their child may be based on their intimate knowledge of their child, whilst professionals may have lower expectations based on their general experience of students with disabilities. In essence, conflicts about perception of "reality" stem from either a professional's failure to do a comprehensive individual assessment of a child or parents' inability to be sufficiently objective in their assessment.

As has already become apparent throughout this book, religious codes, social and political pressures and questionable attitudes to disability are likely to affect many parents of young people with disabilities. Society also gives out messages of being a "good parent" but offers little help in defining exactly what that means. Many parents feel anxious about "doing it right". Recognition of the need to develop parenting skills within the curriculum is increasing, but for existing parents this did not happen.

Added to the possible stress involved in having a child with a disability, many parents need to juggle time between their able-bodied and disabled children. Most families with at least one family member with a disability, are likely to experience practical difficulties with fitting in everything that needs to be done every day. To reiterate, somewhat paradoxically, it is more time-consuming at first to encourage a young person to become more independent than it is to provide total care. When there are other children within the family and family members in full-time employment, it can be extremely difficult to make time to enable a possibly resistant adolescent to do more for herself.

Information is still frequently inaccessible to many parents of young people with disabilities. This inaccessibility is depowering and can mean many parents hold unfounded fears and undue anxiety about their child. It is essential that parents have access to impartial information about service provision and about their rights as parents. Such things as their entitlement to second opinions from consultants and the right to appeal the recommendations of a Statement under Section 7 of the Education Act 1981, is information which parents have a right to know.

STRATEGIES FOR HOME–SCHOOL LIAISON

Having outlined some of the difficulties in home–school relations, which factors can be addressed and overcome within schools?

First and foremost, parents should have a choice as to how they wish to be involved in enabling their children to become more independent. Schools should ask parents if and how they wish to be helped and supported. "Independence training" should start early and there is indisputable benefit in training parents of very young children if they so wish (Leeson and Opolski 1987); be it according to the principles of conductive education (Barker 1984; Caspar 1987) or of behaviour modification (Feldman and Varni 1982; Feldman et al. 1983), or other strategies.

By definition, parents are involved, but if they choose not to co-operate with school programmes, their choice has to be respected and they should be kept informed. However, it is essential that schools, for their part, make active attempts to include parents as part of the team to help young people with disabilities to become more independent. It is best for parents to be involved actively in the assessment and planning of their children's work towards independence at any age, so that they will be able to reinforce at home what is being taught at school. In this way the agreed goals will be more meaningful to them and they will be more committed to the outcomes. To do this, schools need to address the issues of trust and the Blame Game. The rest of this chapter suggests ways that this could be done.

Home–School Liaison Officers

Home–school liaison officers provide a complementary service to Education Welfare Officers, act as links between home and school for the general concerns that may arise. A few special schools visited during this study have part-time home–school liaison officers. These are generally teachers (although occupational therapists, counsellors or social workers would also be appropriate) who have a specified number of hours allocated to visit parents at home. Parents can, if they wish, use some of the time during visits to help them choose the best way to be involved with living skills programmes at school, if at all. Home visits also give the opportunity to assess the physical environment of the home, leading to recommendations for the teaching of maintenance time skills that are relevant to each individual's home environment. It is important that home–school liaison officers are aware that families will differ due to cultural and religious frameworks. It is hoped that this service will be developed, so that a full-time post is provided in all schools. This would involve a full appraisal of the work involved and clarification of this officer's role.

Developing Goals and Contracting

It should be school policy to ask parents to be involved in the discussion and completion of initial assessment and documentation of their child's levels of performance in maintenance time skills. This assessment should form the baseline from which practical goals are developed and parents should have the choice to participate in the development and implementation of these goals. Contracting is a useful tool for implementing goals.

When young people, parents and significant professionals meet to discuss and set realistic goals and define individual roles, each is likely to have more commitment to the desired outcomes. The individual programme plan is a useful complementary tool to contracting as it endeavours to ensure that the young person is receiving planned, consistent intervention.

It is important to bear in mind that practical goals should be realistic. If a child takes two hours to dress without assistance, it would be counter-productive to make this a goal for every morning. It would be more appropriate to set a goal for the child to do this at weekends, and to get ready for bed some evenings when there is more time, if she is not too tired. It should also be remembered that parents have needs too. It is just as important for parents to set goals for themselves, eg. setting time aside to relax. If basic needs such as these are not met, then parents will find it more difficult to empower their children effectively.

Support

Given the mass of conflicting information and misinformation, it would be helpful if parents could have access to support groups and counselling service so that they may feel safe enough to choose to explore what makes them feel, think and act the way they do.

Parent groups offer opportunities for meeting and sharing common concerns with other parents. They are an ideal forum for the discussion of all the issues raised in this book, eg. issues around sexuality. They can either be "self-help" groups or groups run by two experienced group facilitators. Many schools visited during this study have had difficulties setting up these groups, although once set up, they appear to be generally self-perpetuating. Parents should have the option to set the agenda, but it may be helpful to organise the groups around specific topics initially so encouraging parents to participate: the hidden agenda would still be about support if the need is there. Where there are language and cultural differences between parents and professionals, a group facilitated by a bilingual individual who is aware of the particular cultural and disability issues concerned is almost essential (Pilon and Smith 1985).

Counselling can be another invaluable support to some parents. To reiterate, it is essential that anyone taking on a counselling role is adequately trained as counsellor, and it is important that she is aware of her own needs and wider disability issues. It has even been suggested that parent counselling can actually be more helpful in enabling them to become more independent than direct therapy with the young people themselves (Foster *et al.* 1977).

For parents of young people with progressive conditions, research has argued that there is an immense need for more expert family therapeutic intervention:

". . . a strong case could be made for the Local Education Authority to request child guidance consultation services to work with these families through the auspices of the school to which these parents often turned for help." Witte 1985.

Skill Workshops

"Empowering parents with skills to cope, communicate, solve problems, and reach out to others is likely to benefit the entire family." (Kirkham *et al.* 1986).

In the research literature, there is considerable reference to active parental involvement within educational programmes working towards the independence of students. On the whole, parents need to be quite articulate and assertive if they wish to take an active role within programme planning meetings, case reviews and the general transition planning from school. Therefore, it has been argued that some parents should be encouraged to use an advocate at meetings with professionals if they need additional support (Cooper and Bjorling 1981). Researchers and parents' groups have also argued that parents should have access to workshops that facilitate the development of skills to enable them to become more effective members of individual programme planning teams.

The Parent Educational Advocacy Training Center in the USA designs and conducts "educational advocacy courses" for parents of young people with disabilities. These courses are designed to help parents participate effectively in the education system, including referral, evaluation of education,

FIG 10.2: SUMMARY OF NEXT STEPS: A WORKSHOP FOR PARENTS

Roles for Parents	NEXT STEPS
1. Advocates for career education in schools	Self-advocacy and the stages of transition. Balance between vocational and academic curricula. Using individual educational programme plans.
2. Providers of unique information	Developing a profile of children. Learning to to record observation of the child at home. Assertiveness in meetings.
3. Role models	Work options. Improving self-confidence, attitudes and interpersonal skills.
4. Case managers	Identifying needs. Recording progress. Taking notes of meetings and checking that agreements made were acted upon by team members.
5. Risk takers	The skills of letting go. Information about supports available.
6. Financial planners	Information-seeking. Eligibility requirements for assistance. Knowledge of benefits.
7. Programme advocates	Lobbying skills. Influencing positive change in education system.

individual education programmes and post-school placements. The course outlined in Fig 10.2 was developed by and for parents of young people with disabilities aged 14 upwards (Anderson *et al.* 1985). Seven specific roles were identified for parents as their children prepare for the transition from school to an employment setting.

Although this course outline was prepared in America for parents of young people aged 14 and above, the majority of aspects of the course could be usefully adapted for use in Britain with parents of younger children and adolescents, eg. information-seeking skills. Added to this course, it may be helpful to include a workshop on adolescence. In over-simplified terms, this could help parents to gauge whether some of their experiences with their children are more a reflection of adolescence than of their children's disability. In other words, the workshop could help them to put their experiences in perspective.

The issues involved in working with parents to implement the Holographic Model of Living Skills and the implication of it for parents could be a book in its own right. It is hoped that this chapter at least provides a baseline for the development of forums and mechanisms that will allow parents to be effective partners in the education of their children. The notion of empowering young people with disabilities with the skills for becoming more independent presupposes that a similar and concurrent process is taking place with parents. For this, consultation with parents and their active involvement is essential.

CHAPTER ELEVEN
Recommendations

This chapter is divided into two parts:

Recommendations for Action.

Recommendations for Further Research.

RECOMMENDATIONS FOR ACTION

For clarity of presentation, rather than because they are mutually exclusive, the recommendations for action have been broadly divided according to their implications for:

- SCHOOLS
- LOCAL EDUCATION AUTHORITIES
- ISSUES THAT NEED NATIONAL ATTENTION.

SCHOOLS

Curriculum issues

(1) Schools should adopt the consent/choice/autonomy framework for independence and the Holographic Model of Living Skills that puts the framework into operation (see page **18**).

(2) Schools should develop clear working policies on enabling young people with disabilities to become more independent. These should include details of assessment, planning and evaluation procedures (see page **138**).

(3) Schools should develop a cohesive approach to developing independence: linking Personal, Social and Moral Education with "self-care and independence training" (see page **37**).

(4) Schools should teach the skills of "Developing Self", "Learning", "Relating" and "Working and Playing" (see page **40**).

(5) Each student should have an Individual Programme Plan set during regular IPP meetings, using contracting as a planning tool. Each student should develop a personal file of services and options (see page **141**).

(6) Self-Assessment should be seen as an integral part of the curriculum (see page **143**).

(7) Home visits should be conducted so that programmes for teaching maintenance time skills can take account of the home environment. Schools should also have access to a residential resource, so that students can assess, plan and evaluate their maintenance time skills in a suitable residential setting (see page **148**).

(8) School meetings and self-advocacy groups within schools should be developed to give students the opportunity to develop decision-making skills at individual and group level (see page **60**).

(9) Students with disabilities in ordinary schools should have access to individual sessions and/or segregated group work as well as the mainstream curriculum to ensure that individual needs are met (see page **136**).

(10) Students should have the opportunity to go on Outward Bound courses or another form of challenging residential experience (see page **75**).

Administrative Considerations

(11) Each school should identify a multi-disciplinary team to form a living skills curriculum study group, on a voluntary basis (see page **138**).

(12) In-service training for implementing the Holographic Model of Living Skills, under the auspices of staff development workshops should be provided for all staff within the school (see page **147**).

(13) It is essential that schools should have regular multi-disciplinary staff meetings to improve communication between disciplines (see page **139**).

(14) As the model outlined in this book will create additional pressure on staff, it is important for them to receive emotional support and professional guidance individually and in the form of staff support groups (see page **145**).

(15) Each school should employ a home-liaison officer who, with the Education Welfare Officer, would ensure that living skills are taught cohesively in home and school (see page **156**).

(16) Each school should set up parent workshops and/or parent support groups to enhance school–parent relations and the quality of parent involvement (see page **159**).

(17) Link schemes between special and ordinary schools should be established and maintained.

(18) Each school should appoint a co-ordinator for individual programmes (see page **139**).

LOCAL EDUCATION AUTHORITIES (LEAs)

(1) Each LEA should take part in joint service support teams, a substantial proportion of whom should be people with disabilities.

(2) Each LEA should identify named people with disabilities who could work on specific projects, give talks and act as role models within schools.

(3) Adult role models with physical disabilities should be employed within schools, including more professionals with disabilities in key roles (see page **149**).

(4) LEAs should develop and train a pool of non-teaching assistants for students with disabilities in ordinary schools (see page **151**).

(5) Pay scales of non-teaching assistants should be reviewed to take account of their essential role in the Holographic Model.

(6) More male care staff and/or non-teaching assistants should be employed in schools, so that male students can, if they wish, be assisted by male staff (see page **109**).

(7) Measures should be taken to increase the number of school counsellors and occupational therapists working in schools (see page **148**).

ISSUES THAT NEED NATIONAL ATTENTION

WE RECOMMEND THAT:

(1) The Government should set up a National Advisory Council on Special Educational Needs. At least 50% of the council should be people with disabilities and who are experienced in education (see page **150**).

(2) The Government should fund initiatives for the development of living skills curricula for less intellectually able secondary school-aged students.

(3) A national body for "special needs co-ordinators" (co-ordinators of services to students with disabilities in ordinary schools) should be set up to raise awareness, provide and exchange ideas and information.

RECOMMENDATIONS FOR FURTHER RESEARCH

(1) Studies should explore the psychosocial needs of young people with progressive conditions and their families, and ways by which services can meet those needs.

(2) Research should be conducted into the extent and effectiveness of parent workshops, documenting examples of good practice and suggesting strategies for the future.

(3) Research should be conducted into ethnic minority issues within living skills curricula for students with disabilities.

(4) Research should be conducted into profiling and students with disabilities.

(5) Research should be conducted into the assessment of student attitudes and the skills of developing self, learning and relating.

(6) Two sets of curriculum materials derived from this model should be devised:

(i) for all students in ordinary schools, with particular reference to students with disabilities;

(ii) for students with physical disabilities and learning difficulties.

(7) A research study should investigate the feasibility and practicalities of setting up peer counselling services within schools.

APPENDICES

APPENDIX 1:
Useful Resources and Selected Further Reading

This list was compiled from literature searches and from resource lists provided by the University of London Institute of Education, the Family Planning Association (FPA), the schools visited during the study and from an unpublished dissertation by Janet Hughes of St Mary's School, Bexhill-on-Sea, East Sussex "Developing a Life Skills Programme for Children with Special Needs".

We wish to thank all who contributed.

i. LIFESKILLS TEACHING PROGRAMMES

LIFESKILLS TEACHING PROGRAMMES No. 1

Lifeskill: Time management
Lifeskill: How to make and gain from life transitions
Lifeskill: How to be positive about oneself
Lifeskill: How to communicate effectively
Lifeskill: How to be assertive
Lifeskill: How to make, keep and end a relationship
Lifeskill: How to manage negative emotions
Lifeskill: How to find a job

LIFESKILLS TEACHING PROGRAMMES No. 2

Deciding what to teach
Lifeskill: How to study effectively
Lifeskill: How to prevent and manage stress
Lifeskill: How to give and receive feedback
Lifeskill: How to learn from experience
Lifeskill: How to cope with unemployment
Evaluating what we teach

LIFESKILLS TEACHING PROGRAMMES No. 3

Lifeskill: Whole-brain living
Lifeskill: Creative problem-solving
Lifeskill: How to make decisions
Lifeskill: How to be an effective parent of young children

LIFESKILLS TEACHING PROGRAMMES No. 4

Lifeskill: Truth
Lifeskill: Leisure
Lifeskill: Sexism
Lifeskill: Conflict
Lifeskill: Groups and networks
Networks

ii. GENERAL LIVING SKILLS PROGRAMMES

Adland D
GROUPS APPROACH TO DRAMA
Longman 1981

Anderson J
Health Education Authority
HEALTH SKILLS PROJECT
Counselling and Career Development Unit 1988

Baldwin J and Wells H
ACTIVE TUTORIAL WORK – BOOKS 1–6
Blackwell for Lancashire County Council 1984

Bond TIM
GAMES FOR SOCIAL AND LIFE SKILLS
Hutchinson 1985

Brandes D
THE GAMESTERS HANDBOOK TWO
Hutchinson 1982

Brandes D and Ginnis P
A GUIDE TO STUDENT-CENTRED LEARNING
Basil Blackwell 1988

Brown H and Alcoe J
LIFESTYLES: FOR PEOPLE WITH PHYSICAL DISABILITIES
ESCATA
6 Pavilion Parade Brighton BN2 1RA

Dean A and Hegarty S
LEARNING FOR INDEPENDENCE
Further Education Unit (FEU) 1984

Dobinson H M
BASIC SKILLS YOU NEED
Nelson 1984

Dobinson H M
PRACTICE IN GENERAL BASIC SKILLS
Nelson 1984

Hopson B and Scally M
LIFESKILLS TEACHING
Lifeskills Associates 1981

Howard, Joanna
HERE'S HEALTH
Oxford University Press 1985

Jones, March and Watts
LIVING CHOICES
CRAC Life-Style Series 1984

McNicholas J
REAL LIFE READING SKILLS
Scholastic Publications Ltd 1981

Cheston, Molly
IT'S YOUR LIFE
Wheaton (Pergamon Press) 1986

Priestley P and McGuire J
LEARNING TO HELP: BASIC SKILLS EXERCISES
Tavistock Publications

Priestley P, McGuire J, Flegg D, Hemsley V, Welham D
SOCIAL SKILLS AND PERSONAL PROBLEM-SOLVING: A HANDBOOK OF METHODS
Tavistock Publications

Settle, David, & Wise, Charles
CHOICES, MATERIALS & METHODS FOR PSE
Basil Blackwell
108 Cowley Road
Oxford OX4 1JF

Szirom T and Dyson S
GREATER EXPECTATIONS: A SOURCE BOOK FOR WORKING WITH GIRLS AND YOUNG WOMEN
Ed. Slavin H
Lifeskills Associates

ACTIVE TUTORIAL WORK: TRAINING & DISSEMINATION: AN EVALUATION
Basil Blackwell for
Health Education Authority 1985

DEVELOPING PERSONAL EFFECTIVENESS
Careers and Occupational Information Centre (COIC)
Moorfoot
Sheffield S1 4BR

Schools Council/Health Education Council
FIT FOR LIFE
Macmillan Educational 1983

HEALTH AT SCHOOL: CARING FOR THE WHOLE CHILD
Heinemann Nursing 1985

JOINING IN THE COMMUNITY PREPARING FOR FE/ADULT LIFE
Northcote House Publications
Estover Road
Plymouth
PL6 7PZ

LIFEFORCE
Magazine for PSE, Life and Social Skills
Hobsons Publishing PLC

LIFESTYLES: FOR PEOPLE WITH A MENTAL HANDICAP
ESCATA
6 Pavilion Parade
Brighton BN2 1RA

PSE
Films & Videos
Guild Sound & Vision Ltd
6 Royce Road
Peterborough PE1 5YB

PERSONAL & SOCIAL EDUCATION – FAMILY LIFE AND ADOLESCENCE VIDEO
Guild Sound & Vision Ltd
6 Royce Road
Peterborough PE1 5YB

PRACTITIONERS GUIDE NO. 4: PERSONAL EFFECTIVENESS
Department of Employment/Training Agency
Moorfoot
Sheffield S1 4PC

RE & SOCIAL STUDIES INCLUDING PREJUDICE
Mary Glasgow Publications Ltd
Brookhampton Lane
Kineton
Warwick CV35 0JB

SCREENLINK TO PERSONAL AND SOCIAL EDUCATION
Video materials for use in lower and upper secondary school
Pergamon Educational Publications

SKILLS FOR LIVING SET
Spirit Masters Series
Macdonald Educational 1982

SKILLS FOR SCHOOL LEAVERS WITH LEARNING DIFFICULTIES
Department of Employment/Training Agency (COIC)
Moorfoot
Sheffield S1 4PQ

Books for pupil use

Cheston M
IT'S YOUR LIFE: A PERSONAL &
SOCIAL COURSE
Wheaton 1984

Black M
SO YOU WANT TO . . .
    GET ALONG WITH PEOPLE
    BE HAPPY AT WORK
    STAND ON YOUR OWN FEET
    GET A GOOD JOB
    GET STARTED
    GET AROUND
A SET OF WORKBOOKS
Longman 1981

Gowar M
STARTING OUT
Collins 1984

Howard J
HERE'S HEALTH
Oxford University Press 1985

Keyte P
THINGS YOU NEED TO KNOW
Oxford University Press 1985

FIND OUT FOR YOURSELF
The Basic Skills Unit (COIC)
Department of Employment/Training Agency
Moorfoot, Sheffield

Books for pupils with moderate learning difficulties

Prepared by The Home Office Unit for Educational Methods

Barnes D
PERSONAL AND SOCIAL EDUCATION IN SPECIAL SCHOOLS
Pastoral-Care – November 1986

Cleaton D
EXERCISES IN CAREER EDUCATION
Careers Consultants Ltd 1976

Ellis J & Barnes T
LIFE SKILLS TRAINING MANUAL
Community Service Volunteers 1983

McGregor L, Tate M, Robinson K
LEARNING THROUGH DRAMA
Heinemann (for Schools Council) 1980

Perry J
SKILLS FOR ADULT WORKING LIFE: A GUIDE TO RESOURCES
Longman for Schools Council 1984

Ridgeway B
    MATHS ABOUT TOWN
    MATHS FOR EVERYDAY
    MATHS ABOUT THE SHOPS
    MATHS ON THE MOVE
    MATHS FOR LEISURE
    MATHS AT LARGE
    MATHS AT WORK
Edward Arnold

Warren B
DRAMA GAMES
Mencap 1981

Wooster A, *et al.*
PERSONAL AND SOCIAL EDUCATION IN THE SPECIAL SCHOOL: A RESEARCH AND DEVELOPMENT PROJECT
Pastoral Care – November 1986

SKILLS FOR LIVING
    1. BASIC FORM-FILLING
    2. MONEY: HANDLING AND SPENDING
    3. COMMUNICATING
    4. MONEY: SAVING & BUDGETING
    5. SETTLING DOWN
    6. GETTING ABOUT
Macdonald Educational

KEYS TO FORM FILLING
Macmillan 1978

iii. DISABILITY ISSUES

Anderson E M and Clark L
DISABILITY IN ADOLESCENCE
Methuen and Co Ltd 1982

Bowley A and Gardiner L
THE HANDICAPPED CHILD
Churchill Livingstone, 4th ed 1980

Ed. Helen Exley
WHAT IT'S LIKE TO BE ME
Exley Publications Ltd 1984

Gillham B
HANDICAPPING CONDITIONS IN CHILDREN
Croom Helm 1986

Goffman E
STIGMA
Pelican Books 1986

Harns H
PHYSICAL DISABILITY: LIVED EXPERIENCE
London Invalid Children's Aid Association 1983

Jay P
COPING WITH DISABILITY
Disabled Living Foundation 1984

Lonton T and Halliday P
PHYSICALLY DISABLED CHILDREN
Cassell 1988

Male J and Thompson C
THE EDUCATIONAL IMPLICATIONS OF DISABILITY
RADAR 1986

Thomas A *et al.*
PROVISION OF SUPPORT SERVICES FOR THE HANDICAPPED YOUNG ADULT
Charing Cross and Westminster Medical School 1987

Thompson G, Rubin I and Blenker R
COMPREHENSIVE MANAGEMENT OF CEREBRAL PALSY
Academic Press 1983

BEYOND DISABILITY –
THE EMOTIONAL AND SOCIAL DEVELOPMENT OF DISABLED PERSONS
Health Education Bureau 1982

IN OUR OWN RIGHT
Community Service Volunteers (CSV) 1986

WHO ARE YOU STARING AT?
CSV
1980

Self Advocacy

Cooper D, Hersor J
WE CAN CHANGE THE FUTURE: SELF ADVOCACY FOR PEOPLE WITH LEARNING DIFFICULTIES: A STAFF TRAINING RESOURCE
Skill – National Bureau for Students with Disabilities 1986

Gould M and McTaggart N
SELF ADVOCACY FOR TRANSITION: IMPLICATIONS OF STUDENT LEADERSHIP POTENTIAL TODAY
Self Advocacy Training Project of Maryland 1988.

iv. DEVELOPING SELF

Anderson F J
Self-Concept and Coping in Adolescents with a Physical Disability
ISSUES IN MENTAL HEALTH NURSING 1982 Vol 4, p. 257–274

Bluebond M and Langer M
THE PRIVATE WORLDS OF DYING CHILDREN
Princeton University Press 1977

Burns R
SELF-CONCEPT, DEVELOPMENT AND EDUCATION
Holt 1982

Burton L
CARE OF THE CHILD FACING DEATH
Routledge 1974

Hurt A
Adolescence and Physical Impairment: an interactionist view
In: Barton L and Tomlinson S
SPECIAL EDUCATION AND SOCIAL INTERESTS
Croom Helm 1984

Jewett C
HELPING CHILDREN COPE WITH SEPARATION AND LOSS
Batsford Academic

Kashani J H
Self Esteem of Handicapped Children and Adolescents
DEVELOPMENTAL MEDICINE AND CHILD NEUROLOGY 1986

Kessel M *et al.*
Adventure Etc – A Health Promotion Program for Chronically Ill and Disabled Youth
J OF ADOLESCENT HEALTH CARE 1985 Vol 6, p. 433–438

Kubler Ross E
ON DEATH AND DYING
Tavistock 1969

Nicholas F M
COPING WITH CONFLICT: A RESOURCE BOOK FOR THE MIDDLE SCHOOL YEARS
Lifeskills Associates 1988

Ostering H and Nieminen S
Concept of Self and the attitude of CP children towards their handicap
INTERNATIONAL JOURNAL REHAB RESEARCH 1982 Vol 5 (2), pp. 235–237

Ward B and Houghton J
GOOD GRIEF
Cruse 1987

Willian-Worden J
GRIEF COUNSELLING AND GRIEF THERAPY
Tavistock Publications

Woodburn S
THE SOCIAL IMPLICATIONS OF SPINA BIFIDA
NFER/Nelson 1985

Wright B
PHYSICAL DISABILITY: A PSYCHO-SOCIAL APPROACH
1980

Books for Bereaved Children

Althea
WHEN UNCLE BOB DIED
Dinosaur Publications 1982

Mildred Kantrowitz
WHEN VIOLET DIED
Bodley Head 1983

T Madler
WHY DID GRANDMA DIE?

Developing Sexuality

Babuscio J
WE SPEAK FOR OURSELVES
SPCK Publications

The Clarity Collective
TAUGHT NOT CAUGHT
Learning Development Aids 1983

Craft A
MENTAL HANDICAP AND
SEXUALITY: ISSUES AND
PERSPECTIVE
Costello 1987

Craft A and Craft M
SEX EDUACTION AND
COUNSELLING FOR MENTALLY
HANDICAPPED PEOPLE
Costello 1983

Davies M
SEX EDUCATION FOR YOUNG
PEOPLE WITH A PHYSICAL
DISABILITY
SPOD 1982

Eds: Dechesne BHH, Pons C and
Schellen MCM
SEXUALITY AND HANDICAP
Woodhead-Faulkner 1985

Greengross W
ENTITLED TO LOVE
National Marriage Guidance Council
and National Fund for Research into
Crippling Diseases
Malby Press 1976

Haight S L and Fachting D D
*Material for Teaching Sexuality, Love
and Maturity to High School Students
with Learning Disabilities*
J OF LEARNING DISABILITIES Vol
19 no 6, June/July 1986

Hamre-Nietupski S and Ford A
*Sex Education and Related Skills: A
Series of Programs Implemented with
Severely Handicapped Students*
SEXUALITY AND DISABILITY Vol
4 No 3 1981

Newman B
SEX FOR YOUNG PEOPLE WITH
SPINA BIFIDA OR CEREBRAL
PALSY
ASBAH 1983

Stewart W F R
THE SEXUAL SIDE OF HANDICAP
Woodhead-Faulkner 1979

LIKE OTHER PEOPLE
(video)
Producer: SPOD

SEXUALITY AND DISABILITY
(video)
Brook Advisory Centre, Education and
Publication Unit

SEXUALITY AND THE
PHYSICALLY DISABLED – AN
INTRODUCTION FOR
COUNSELLORS
SPOD 1982

v. LEARNING

Darnborough A and Kinrade D
DIRECTORY FOR DISABLED
PEOPLE
(fifth edition) Woodhead-Faulkner in
association with RADAR 1988

vi. RELATING

Dickson A
A WOMAN IN YOUR OWN RIGHT
Quartet Books 1985

Jones R N
*Relationship Skills Training in Schools:
Some Fieldwork Observations*
B JOURNAL OF GUIDANCE AND
COUNSELLING
Vol 14 No 3 Sept 1986

Townsend A
ASSERTION TRAINING: A
HANDBOOK FOR TRAINERS
FPA Education Unit 1985

vii. WORKING AND PLAYING

Carruthers C
LIFESKILLS MANUAL – PERSONAL CARE
Winslow Press 1987

Male J and Ward J
WORKING TOGETHER TOWARDS INDEPENDENCE
RADAR 1987

McCarthy B P
DISABLED EVE: AIDS IN MENSTRUATION
Disabled Living Foundation 1981

Turnbull P and Ruston R
CLOTHES SENSE FOR DISABLED PEOPLE OF ALL AGES
Disabled Living Foundation 1985

Whelan E and Speake B
LEARNING TO COPE
Human Horizons 1979

Wighton J, Ed: Mercer A
COOKERY: MEALS FOR ONE
Winslow Press 1984

EQUIPMENT FOR THE DISABLED
Series from Mary Malborough Lodge
(see Directory for Disabled People)

Health Management

Picton M
UNDERSTANDING HEALTH & SAFETY
Blackie & Son 1981

HERE'S HEALTH
Community Service Volunteers
1987

Leisure Time Skills

Ed: Nicholas Gair
THE DUKE OF EDINBURGH'S AWARD HANDBOOK
The Duke of Edinburgh's Award 1988

viii. CHECKLISTS

Dorothy J and Cheseldine S
PATHWAYS TO INDEPENDENCE
Hodder & Stoughton 1982

Felce D, Jenkins J, de Kock U, Mansell J
THE BEREWEEKE SKILL-TEACHING SYSTEM: GOAL-SETTING CHECKLIST FOR ADULTS
National Foundation for Educational Research/Nelson 1986

Whelen E, Speake B and Strickland T
THE COPEWELL CURRICULUM
The Further Education Unit 1984

Whitehouse J
Mossford Assessment Chart for the Physically Handicapped
NFER – Nelson 1983

ix. PARENTS

Anderson W et al.
"Planning for employment: a workshop for parents"
COALITION QUARTERLY
Vol 4 No 4 1985

Leeson J and Opolski J
"Parents and Professionals: A Working Relationship"
EARLY CHILD DEVELOPMENT AND CARE Vol 27 1987

Mitler P and McConachie M
PARENTS, PROFESSIONALS AND MENTALLY HANDICAPPED PEOPLE
Croom Helm 1983

Pugh G
PARENTS AS PARTNERS
National Children's Bureau 1981

Szwed C
"Sharing the Caring: a discussion of home/school liaison"
PASTORAL CARE June 1986

Wolfendale S
PARENTS' PARTICIPATION IN CHILDREN'S DEVELOPMENT AND EDUCATION
Gordon and Breach 1983

x. STAFF DEVELOPMENT AND PROGRAMME EVALUATION

Brearley G and Birchcley P
INTRODUCING COUNSELLING SKILLS AND TECHNIQUES WITH PARTICULAR APPLICATION FOR THE PARAMEDICAL PROFESSIONS
Faber and Faber 1986

Duncan J
"Caring for the Pastoral Carers"
PASTORAL CARE – February 1987

Ed: Hegarty S and Moses O
DEVELOPING EXPERTISE – INSET FOR SPECIAL EDUCATIONAL NEEDS
NFER – Nelson 1988

Lawley P
"The Pastoral Care of Teachers"
PASTORAL CARE – November 1985

Lowe P
Special Needs in Ordinary Schools
RESPONDING TO ADOLESCENT NEEDS: A PASTORAL CARE APPROACH
Cassell 1988

McBrien J and Foxen T
EDUCATION FOR THE DEVELOPMENTALLY YOUNG (EDY)
IN – SERVICE COURSE FOR MENTAL HANDICAP PRACTICTIONERS
Manchester University Press 1984

Oxon H
OPTIONS FOR CHANGE: A STAFF TRAINING HANDBOOK ON PERSONAL RELATIONSHIPS AND SEXUALITY FOR PEOPLE WITH A MENTAL HANDICAP
Family Planning Association Education Unit, 1986

APPENDIX 2:
Useful Addresses

General Organisations

Association of Charity Officers
c/o RICS Benevolent Fund
2nd Floor
Tavistock House North
Tavistock Square
London WC1H 9RH
01 387 0578

Association of Child Psychotherapists
Burgh House
New End Square
London NW3 1LT
01 794 8881

Association of Paediatric Chartered
Physiotherapists
3 Stanley Gardens
Sanderstead
South Croydon
Surrey CR2 9AH

Association of Swimming Therapy
Treetops
Swan Hill
Ellesmere
Salop SY12 0LZ
069 171 3542

British Homeopathic Association
27a Devonshire Street
London W1 1RJ
01 935 2163

British Society for Music Therapy
69 Avondale Avenue
East Barnet
Hertfordshire EN4 8NB
01 368 8879

Brook Advisory Services
Education and Publications Unit
24 Albert Street
Birmingham B4 7UD
021 643 1554

Centre for Learning to Learn More
Effectively
636 Wilmslow Road
Didsbury
Manchester M20 0AH
061 445 2411

Child Accident Prevention Trust
75 Portland Place
London W1N 3AL
01 636 2545

Child Poverty Action Group
1–5 Bath Street
London EC1V 9PY
01 253 3404

Children's Legal Centre
20 Compton Terrace
London N1 2UN
01 359 6251/2

College of Speech Therapists
Harold Poster House
Lechmere Road
London NW2 5BU
01 459 8521

Compassionate Friends
National Office
6 Denmark Street
Bristol BS1 5DQ
0272 292778

Community Service Volunteers (CSV)
237 Pentonville Road
London N1 9NJ
01 278 6601

Counselling and Career Development
University of Leeds
Unit (CCDU)
44 Clarendon Road
Leeds LS2 9PJ
0532 334911

Cruse: National Organisation for the Widowed and their children
Cruse House
126 Sheen Road
Richmond
Surrey TW9 1UR
01 940 4818/9047

Duke of Edinburgh's Award
5 Prince of Wales Terrace
Kensington
London W8 5PG
01 937 5205

Equal Opportunities Commission
Overseas House
Quay Street
Manchester M3 3HN
061 833 9244

Family Planning Association (FPA)
St Andrew's House
27–35 Mortimer Street
London W1N 7RJ
01 636 7866

Further Education Unit (FEU)
Elizabeth House
York Road
London SE1 7PH

Health Education Authority
Hamilton House
Mabledon Place
London WC1H 9TX
01 631 0930

Lifeskills Associates
Clarendon Chambers
51 Clarendon Road
Leeds
LS2 9NZ
0532 467128

National Association of Young People's
Counselling and Advisory Services
17–23 Albion Street
Leicester LE1 6GD

National Foundation for Educational
Research in England and Wales – NFER
The Mere
Upton Park
Slough
Berks SL1 2DQ

National Council of Voluntary
Organisations (NCVO)
26 Bedford Square
London WC1B 3HU
01 636 4066

Pre-School Playgroups Association
61–63 Kings Cross Road
London WC1X 9LL
01 833 0991

Proctor & Gamble Educational Service
PO Box 15H
Newgate House
Newcastle Upon Tyne NE99 1SH

Society of Horticultural Therapy
Goulds Ground
Vallis Way
Frome
Somerset BA11 3DW
0373 64782

TACADE
3rd Floor Furness House
Trafford Road
Salford
061 848 0351

Women's Health Information Centre
52 Featherstone Street
London EC1Y 8RT
01 251 6580

Women's Therapy Centre
6 Manor Gardens
London N7 6LA
01 263 6200

Disability Organisations

81 Action (National Network of Parents of Children with Special Educational Needs)
52 Magnaville Road
Bishops Stortford
Hertfordshire CM23 4DW

Advisory Centre for Education (ACE)
18 Victoria Park Square
London E2 9BP
01 980 4596 (afternoons only)

Advocacy Alliance
115 Golden Lane
London EC1Y 0TJ
01 253 2056

Arthritis Care
6 Grosvenor Crescent
London SW1
01 235 0902

Artsline
5 Crowndale Road
London NW1 1TJ
01 388 2227

Association for All Speech Impaired Children (AFASIC)
347 Central Markets
London EC1A 9NH
01 236 3632/6487

Association of Disabled Professionals
The Stables
73 Pound Road
Banstead
Surrey SM7 2HU
0737 352366

Association of Parents of Vaccine-Damaged Children
2 Church Street
Shipston-on-Stour
Warwickshire CV36 4AP
0608 61595

Association for Spina Bifida and Hydrocephalus (ASBAH)
22 Upper Woburn Place
London WC1H 0EP
01 388 1382/8

Asthma Society
St Thomas's Hospital
Lambeth Palace Road
London SE1 7EH
01 928 9292

Banstead Mobility Centre
Park Road
Burgh Heath
Banstead
Surrey
0737 351674

Barnardo's
Tanners Lane
Barkingside
Essex IG6 1QG
01 550 8822

British Amputee Sports Association
Harvey Road
Aylesbury
Bucks HP21 9PP
0296 27889

British Council of Organisations of
Disabled People (BCODP)
Long Close
Cemetery Lane
Ripley
Derbyshire DE5 3HY
0773 570132

British Diabetic Association
10 Queen Anne Street
London W1M 0BD
01 323 1531

British Epilepsy Association
Ansley House
40 Hanover Square
Leeds LS3 1BE
0532 439 393

British Institute of Mental Handicap
(BIMH)
Information and Resource Centre
Wolverhampton Road
Kidderminster
Worcester DY10 3PD
0562 850251

British Ski Club for the Disabled
Springmount
Berwick St John
Shaftesbury
Dorset SP7 0HQ
0747 188515

British Sports Association for the
Disabled
34 Osnaburgh Street
London NW1 3ND
01 383 7277

Brittle Bone Society
Unit 4, Block 20
112 City Road
Calunie Road
Dunsinane Industrial Estate
Dundee DD2 3QT
0382 817771

Calibre (Cassette Library for the Blind
and Handicapped)
Aylesbury
Buckinghamshire HP22 5XQ
0296 432339/81211

Calvert Trust Adventure Centre for
Disabled People
Little Crosthwaite
Under Skiddaw
Keswick
Cumbria CA12 4QD
07687 72254

Campaigns for People
with Mental Handicaps
12a Maddox Street
London W1R 9PL
01 491 0727

Camping for the Disabled
20 Burton Close
Dawley
Telford
Shropshire TF4 2BX
0952 507653

Carers National Association
29 Chilworth Mews
London W2 3RG
01 724 7776

Castle Priory College
Thames Street
Wallingford
Oxon OX10 0HE
0491 37551

Centre on Environment for the
Handicapped (CEH)
35 Great Smith Street
London SW1P 3BJ
01 222 7980

Centre for Studies in Integration and Education
4th Floor
415 Edgware Road
London NW2 6NB
01 425 8642

Concord Video & Film Council Ltd
201 Felixstowe Road
Ipswich
Suffolk 1P3 9BJ
0473 726012

Contact a Family
16 Strutton Ground
Victoria
London SW1P 2HP
01 222 2695/3969

Creative Young People Together (CRYPT)
Forum Workspace
Stirling Road
Chichester
West Sussex PO19 2EN
0243 786064

Crohn's in Childhood Research Appeal
Parkgate House
35b West Barnes Lane
Motspur Park
Surrey KT3 6NB
01 949 6209

Cystic Fibrosis Research Trust
Alexandra House
5 Blythe Road
Bromley
Kent BR1 3RS
01 464 7211

Development Trust for the Young Disabled
RHHI – Royal Hospital and Home for Incurables
West Hill Putney
London SW15 3SW
01 788 4511

Disability Alliance
25 Denmark Street
London WC2H 8NJ
01 240 0806

Disabled Income Group (DIG)
Millmead Business Centre
Millmead Road
London N17 9QU
01 801 8013

Disabled Living Foundation
380–384 Harrow Road
London W9 2HU
01 289 6111

Equipment for the Disabled
Mary Marlborough Lodge
Nuffield Orthopaedic Centre
Headington
Oxford OX3 7LD
0865 750103

Family Fund
PO Box 50
York YO1 1UY
0904 21115

Federation of London Dial-A-Rides
St Margarets
25 Leighton Road
London NW5 2QD
01 482 2325

Friedrich's Ataxia Group
The Common
Cranleigh
Surrey GU6 8SB
0483 272741

Gay Men's Disabled Club
c/o Gay's the Word
66 Marchmont Street
London WC1N 1AB

GEMMA (Lesbians with/without disabilities)
BM Box 5700
London WC1N 3XX

GRAEAE
The Diorama
14 Peto Place
London NW1 4LH
01 935 5588

Haemophilia Society
123 Westminster Bridge Road
London SE1 7HR
01 928 2020

Handicapped Children's Adventure
Playground Association
Fulham Palace Playground
Bishops Avenue
London SW6 6EA
01 731 2753

Handicapped Persons Research Unit
Newcastle Upon Tyne Polytechnic
No 1 Coach Lane
Coach Lane Campus
Newcastle Upon Tyne NE7 7TW
091 235 8211

Headway
(National Head Injuries Association)
200 Mansfield Road
Nottingham NG1 3HX
0602 622382

International Cerebral Palsy Society
5a Netherhall Gardens
London NW3 5RN
01 794 9761

Invalid Children's Aid Nationwide
(ICAN)
Allen Graham House
198 City Road
London EC1V 2PH
01 608 2462

John Groom's Association for the
Disabled
10 Gloucester Drive
Finsbury Park
London N4 2LP
01 802 7272

King's Fund Centre
126 Albert Street
Camden Town
London NW1 7NF
01 267 6111

Lady Hoare Trust for Physically
Disabled Children
7 North Street
Midhurst
West Sussex GU29 9DJ
073081 3696

Leukaemia Care Society
PO Box 82
Exeter EX2 5DP
0392 218514

Mencap
123 Golden Lane
London EC1Y 0RT
01 253 9433

Mobility Information Service
Unit 2a
Atcham Industrial Estate
Upton Magna
Shrewsbury SY4 4UG
0743 77489

Motability
Gate House
Westgate
Harlow
Essex CM20 1HR
0279 635666

Motor Neurone Disease Association
61 Derngate
Northampton NN1 1UE
0604 22269/250505

Muscular Dystrophy Group of Great
Britain and Northern Ireland
Nattrass House
35 Macauley Road
London SW4 0QP
01 720 8055

National Association for Limbless
Disabled (NALD)
31 The Mall
London W5 2PX
01 579 1758/9

National Association for the Welfare of
Children in Hospital (NAWCH)
Argyle House
29–31 Euston Road
London NW1
01 833 2041

National Council for Special Education
1 Wood Street
Stratford Upon Avon
Warwickshire CV37 6JE
0789 205332

National Federation of Gateway Clubs
123 Golden Lane
London EC1Y 0RY
01 253 9433

National Library for the Handicapped
Child
University of London Institute of
Education
20 Bedford Way
London WC1H 0AL
01 636 1500 ext 599

Physically Handicapped and Able-
Bodied (PHAB)
Tavistock House North
Tavistock Square
London WC1H 9HX
01 388 1963

Opportunities for the Disabled
1 Bank Buildings
Princes Street
London EC2R 8EU
01 726 4961

Play Matters (formerly National Toy
Libraries Association)
68 Church Way
London NW1 1LT
01 387 9592

Queen Elizabeth's Foundation for the
Disabled
Leatherhead
Surrey KT22 0BN
037 284 2204

RADAR
25 Mortimer Street
London W1N 8AB
01 637 5400

Rehabilitation Engineering Movement
Advisory Panel (REMAP) (Part of
RADAR)
25 Mortimer Street
London W1N 8AB
01 637 5400

Royal London Society for the Blind
105–109 Salusbury Road
London NW6 6RH
01 624 8844

Shape
1 Thorpe Close
London W10 5XL
01 960 9245

Skills for People
Haldane House
Tankerville Terrace
Jesmond
Newcastle Upon Tyne
NE2 3AH
091 281 8737

SKILL – National Bureau for Students
with Disabilities (formerly NBHS)
336 Brixton Road
London SW9 7AA
01 274 0565

Spinal Injuries Association (SIA)
Yeoman's House
76 St James's Lane
Muswell Hill
London N10 3DF
01 444 2121

SPOD (Association to Aid the Sexual
and Personal Relationships of People
with a Disability)
286 Camden Road
London N7 0BJ
01 607 8851/2

Tripscope (Transport Information for
People with Disability)
63 Esmond Road
London W4 1JE
01 994 9294

Voluntary Council for Handicapped
Children
8 Wakley Street
London EC1V 7QE
01 278 9441

Wales Council for the Disabled
Caerbragdy Industrial Estate
Bedwas Road
Caerphilly
Mid Glamorgan
CF8 3SL
0222 887325

Genetic Counselling Centres

Department of Clinical Genetics
Institute of Child Health
30 Guildford Street
London WC1

Department of Genetic Counselling
Addenbrookes Hospital
Hills Road
Cambridge CB2 2QQ

Department of Medical Genetics
Old Road
Headington
Oxford OX3 7LE

Department of Medical Genetics
St Mary's Hospital
Hathersage Road
Manchester M13 0JH

Muscle Clinic
Regional Neurological Centre
Newcastle General Hospital
Westgate Road
Newcastle Upon Tyne
NE4 6BE

Section of Medical Genetics
Department of Medicine
University Hospital of Wales
Heath Park
Cardiff CF4 4XW

American Disability Organisations

National Information Center for
Handicapped Children and Youth
(NICHCY)
PO Box 1492
Washington DC 20013
USA

People First of Oregon
PO Box 12642
Salem, OR 97309

People First of Washington
PO Box 381
Tacoma WA 98401

Self-Advocacy Training Project of
Maryland
3000 Chestnut Avenue #204
Baltimore
Maryland 21211
USA

World Institute on Disability
1720 Oregon Street
Suite 4
Berkeley
California
USA

Communication Aids Centres – England and Wales

Jayne Easton
Communication Aids Centre
Frenchay Hospital
Frenchay
Bristol BS16 1LE

Communication Aids Centre
Southampton General Hospital
Tremona Road
Southampton SO9 4XY

Nicola Jolleff
Communication Aids Centre
The Wolfson Centre
Mecklenburgh Square
London WC1N 2AP

Julia Le Patourel
Communication Aids Centre
Charing Cross Hospital
Fulham Palace Road
London W6 8RF

Elspeth Middleton
Communication Aids Assessment Centre
Treliske Hospital
Truro
Cornwall

Liz Panton
Communication Aids Centre
The Dene Centre
Castles Farm Road
Newcastle Upon Tyne NE3 1PH

Carol Thomas-Wyllie
Communication Aids Centre
Rookwood Hospital
Fairwater Road
Llandaff
Cardiff CF5 2YN

Brigid Fisher
Leicester Communication Aids
Information and Resource Centre
Speech Therapy Department
Yeoman House
5a Yeoman Street
Leicester LE1 1UF

APPENDIX 3:
Paradigm Shift

THE INDUSTRIAL ERA PARADIGM IS GIVING WAY TO THE INFORMATION ERA PARADIGM

LEARNING

Industrial Era Paradigm

- Emphasis on learning facts.
- Educational institutions were hierarchical, demanding conformity of thinking and behaviour.
- Prescribed curriculum, nationally dictated.
- Heavy labelling of people, eg. ESN, gifted, maladjusted.
- Concern with achieving norms.
- Left-brain focus in content and process of teaching.
- Emphasis on abstract knowledge.
- Parents and the community are kept at a distance.
- Education only comes with schooling, in the early years of life.
- Didactic.
- Either/or.
- Yes but . . .

Information Era Paradigm

- Emphasis on learning how to learn.
- Learning relationships are two-way with an emphasis away from formalised roles like teacher and student to one of people working together to discover and learn.
- Negotiated curriculum, determined locally.
- Minimal labelling.
- Concern with achieving excellence and high performance.
- Whole-brain focus.
- Concrete experience and skills valued as highly as knowledge.
- Community input encouraged.
- Education is life-long.
- Participative.
- Multiple options.
- Yes and . . .

RELATIONSHIPS

Industrial Era Paradigm

- Rigid sex-role differentiation.
- Value of relationships judged by their length of time.
- One marriage for life.
- People related to according to hierarchical status.

Information Era Paradigm

- Behaviour determined by needs, skills and interests, not by gender.
- Value measured by the quality of the experience.
- Many options – one marriage, serial marriage, living together, singles households, homosexual "marriage".
- Emphasis on networking between peers.

Reproduced from:
Lifeskills Teaching Programmes No. 3 page 16
B Hopson and M Scally
Lifeskills Associates 1987

APPENDIX 3: (continued)
Paradigm Shift

THE INDUSTRIAL ERA PARADIGM IS GIVING WAY TO THE INFORMATION ERA PARADIGM

WORKING AND PLAYING		DEVELOPING SELF AND OTHERS	
Industrial Era Paradigm	**Information Era Paradigm**	**Industrial Era Paradigm**	**Information Era Paradigm**
• People have to fit into jobs – high emphasis on selection and training.	• Jobs are fitted to people – emphasis on negotiation.	• Help is provided by institutions and professionals.	• Self-help networks.
• Organisations are hierarchical with authority emphasised.	• Organisations are "flatter" with an emphasis on worker participation.	• Conformity and adjustment valued.	• Plurality and innovation valued.
• A job for life is the goal.	• People have a variety of jobs and occupations.	• Emphasis on eliminating disease.	• Emphasis on achieving "wellness".
• The 48-48-48 model (48 hrs a week, 48 weeks a year, 48 years of your life).	• A variety of alternative career patterns.	• Advice and directed help.	• Counselling and advocacy.
• Work = a job = income.	• Work can be paid or unpaid. Income comes from more than one source.	• Problems are to be eliminated.	• Problems are normal, challenging and are to be welcomed.
• Competition encouraged.	• Co-operation encouraged.	• Change should be minimised.	• Change should be managed.
• Work and play are separate.	• The two become increasingly blurred.	• Transitions can be harmful.	• Transitions offer opportunities for growth.
• Stability and security are the two predominant "drivers".	• The desire for change and growth are the two predominant "drivers".	• Negative feelings are to be suppressed.	• Negative feelings are to be used constructively.
• Career development is vertical only.	• "Up is not the only way" summarises the variety of acceptable career patterns.		
• Job-centred.	• Balanced lifestyle.		

Reproduced from:
Lifeskills Teaching Programmes No. 3 page 16
B Hopson and M Scally
Lifeskills Associates 1987

APPENDIX 4:
"Through the Looking Glass" – Reflections on Reality

Written and delivered by Gill Brearly – National Council for Special Education – Annual Conference 1982 at Guy's Hospital, London.

When considering the skills needed for a life that has what I would consider acceptable qualities, I found I was falling easily into considering the quality of life of a person with a disability. Does this mean that I have a different standard of values for my own life?

I am reminded of the White Queen in Lewis Carroll's book, the title of which I have used for this talk. The White Queen stated:

"SOMETIMES I HAVE BELIEVED AS MANY AS SIX IMPOSSIBLE THINGS BEFORE BREAKFAST."

It is difficult for me to believe that, as a passionate advocate of integration for people with disabilities, I was reverting to thinking of "them". Impossible to believe that I could fall so easily into denigrating the expectations of people with disabilities. However, I intend to follow the White Queen's example and attempt to believe a few impossible things.

Carl Whitaker, family therapist, says that "The only you I know is me". I believe this with no difficulty, and make no apology for telling you some of my thoughts about my attitudes and about those I see reflected around me. To do this, I will need to use words Humpty Dumpty said to Alice:

"WHEN I USE A WORD IT MEANS JUST WHAT I CHOOSE IT TO MEAN – NEITHER MORE NOR LESS."

I would prefer to talk to you in Blissymbols, as do a number of the children I work with. Blissymbols are direct and unequivocal, although capable of great subtlety. However, I would risk your being so taken aback and threatened by such an unusual means of communication that you would block your ability to understand me, as happens to a number of the children with whom I work. So I need to use words.

I will try to use simple and direct words so that communication exists between us. Jargon may sometimes be useful when two people who use the same jargon are communicating, but jargon is by its very nature exclusive – and therefore excluding. I will try to avoid jargon. It seems to me to be a vital need for everyone involved in Education for Living to communicate. If parents, physiotherapists, families, teachers, relatives, social workers, young people, all the other many, many people who contribute are not able to communicate directly and with clarity, we have failed at the very first challenge.

The first thoughts I want to share are summarised by the Red Queen:

"WHAT IS THE USE OF A CHILD WITHOUT ANY MEANING?".

My child has meaning. My child is myself given another chance. My child is hope for the future. My child is joy and learning and sharing, giving and receiving. My child gives me endless fascination in observing her learning and her discovery, great pride in her achievements. My child means that my role, my identity, my worth, is assured.

My child is not disabled.

What, I wonder, is the meaning to us of a severely damaged child?

I do not know exactly what the meaning of the word "handicap" is, or if I accept it.

I do know that I cannot and will not accept disability, that a potentially whole child can be born irreparably damaged or that an able person can be deprived of, bereaved of, his wholeness.

However, I can accept people with disabilities. This acceptance of a person, while refusing to accept the disabilities, may sound impossible but I can do it. This is the reason for what may appear a somewhat pedantic refusal to use the phrase "disabled person" instead of "a person with a disability". Putting the person first, trying to remember always to use that form of reference, does influence the way I think. It is easy for me to say, for example, that in our school we have one-third cerebral palsies, one-third spina bifidas, one-sixth muscular dystrophies and one-sixth other handicaps. It is easy, and it can effectively protect me from remembering, that one hundred and thirty-one children are growing up with disabling illnesses or deformities.

A Gnat remarked to Alice:

"WHAT'S THE USE OF THEIR HAVING NAMES IF THEY WON'T ANSWER TO THEM?".

I am sure you all know that a typical spastic cerebral palsy is slow in grasping new ideas, is easily confused and needs a great deal of reinforcement.

Hydrocephalic spina bifidas show typical learning problems related to perceptual disorders.

Hemiplegics are prone to disruptive behaviour.

Teachers can never resist lecturing.

Social workers are woolly minded idealists.

Physiotherapists are hearty types.

We don't all answer to our names when stereotypes are the names we are called by. It is sometimes difficult to separate the clinical symptoms of a condition with the behaviour of an individual person who suffers from that condition.

I find that I have to continually remind myself that my non-handicapped daughters displayed patterns of behaviour during their normal development, that mirror "problems" associated with disability that can make me unthinkingly decide that a child is behaving abnormally. Johnnie's tantrums, obstructive behaviour and disinclination to study may be clear symptoms of the handicap of adolescence, and I need to know Johnnie as a person rather than as a hemiplegic in order to best help him.

Alice defends an accusation of being a myth by saying:

"IF I WASN'T REAL, I WOULDN'T BE ABLE TO CRY."

As a teacher of the physically handicapped and as a physiotherapist, I have been told, "Don't get involved".

If I prevent myself from becoming involved with the people with whom I work, if I do not allow myself to be moved by them, then I am functioning as less than a whole person. I am being unreal.

To be real is frightening. I might be hurt. Demands may be made on me. I may have to face my own inadequacies.

I live in a real world. Refusing to be real with people who are disabled is to deny that they belong in my real world. I cannot then use phrases like, "Face up to reality", "They need to learn to cope with real life", "Education for Life", because I will not allow people with disabilities to share my real world.

So I will get involved. I will be real. I will cry, rage, rejoice and be who I am.

There is nothing like it.

"I DIDN'T SAY THERE WAS NOTHING BETTER. I SAID THERE WAS NOTHING LIKE IT". I reflect the White Knight's words.

I live in a real world, and part of my real world involves work in special education: and special education is in many ways a looking glass world.

Two remarks overheard in the staff room illustrate this:

"I've just had to tick Richard off for running in the corridor. Isn't it fantastic, he's doing *so* well."

"You'll never guess what's just happened – I never thought I'd ever achieve it – Mark – yes, *Mark* – told me to go away!".

Special education is a looking glass world where it can be an insurmountable struggle for an adolescent to rebel. How does a child who is dependent on adults for his physical care rebel, test his independence, establish himself as a person? How does a child who needs help with her personal care, test her reality, establish her own personality, become real?

Alice said of Looking Glass Land:

"THE BOOKS ARE SOMETHING LIKE OUR BOOKS, ONLY THE WORDS GO THE WRONG WAY."

I work with children who have educational, developmental, emotional, social, mental and physical disabilities. I can only imagine what their world must be like. I can never know.

I live in the real world, whatever that is. I do not want to compound the disabilities of the people with whom I work by refusing to share my world, by withholding what it is like to be me.

Only in this way can I hope to begin to share what it is like for them, so that together we can work out a strategy for education for life in a non-disabled world.

"NOW IF YOU'D ASKED MY ADVICE, I'D HAVE SAID 'LEAVE OFF AT SEVEN'."

I don't know what Humpty Dumpty had in mind, but for me it would be so much easier if all people with disabilities "left off at seven".

I can cope with "the babies".

I can care for, comfort, hope and plan for children with disabilities up to seven years old or thereabouts.

Older than that – adolescent, adult people with disabilities – things are difficult for me.

I can identify too closely with an adult whose mind and soul are trapped in a deformed and uncontrolled body and it scares me.

I am made to feel guilty about my own abilities and some of my joy in my own achievements is spoiled for me.

My own identity is challenged by them. I am proud of my own painful journey towards acceptance of myself. I feel I am at least in sight of my own adulthood, my own maturity. But – if I admit that someone disabled is an adult and can achieve a full maturity, it makes my struggles seem pretty pathetic.

So it is much easier for me to make sure that I am not ever frightened, made to feel guilty or challenged. I can do this fairly effectively by making sure that people with disabilities remain forever children, leaving off at seven.

Children of seven have few opportunities to make choices, need supervision and caring for, have decisions made for them and are seldom consulted about plans for their future.

But I do want children to grow into adults. Can I help them?

Like the White King, perhaps

"I'M GOOD ENOUGH. ONLY I'M NOT STRONG ENOUGH".

I must become aware of where and why my strength is likely to fail. I have my own hidden motives, blocks, fears and resentments that will prevent me from wanting constructively to help the children with whom I work to become adults.

I have said something about my fears and the guilt and negative feelings that may block me. Resentment I am also aware of. There are times when I do resent the fact that a person with a disability can make demands I feel I cannot make. When I am under stress, tired and feeling unappreciated, the "right" of someone who is disabled to have help and sympathy, be cared for and protected, seems very much to be envied. Of course, it is ridiculous to be envious of someone disabled; but I do feel it and I feel denied of the right to feel depressed or sad and to ask for sympathy and help.

So what can I do? Alice could be speaking for a person who is disabled when she says:

"I DON'T LIKE BELONGING TO ANOTHER PERSON'S DREAM".

I must not make agendas for other people. I recently talked with a woman who is a fierce fighter for the rights of disabled people. She asked me how she could *make* people fight for their rights and suggested that people in residential care must be forced to demand these rights. When I suggested that I felt a basic right of every adult was to make their own choices, she wheeled herself away in a rage. I do not want to decide what is "right" for another human being. I want to help people see where and what their choices are, I want people to experience making wrong choices (wrong by the criterion of their needs) and to gain the ability to recognise the choices that there are in every situation. I want to respect the choice that other people make. I want to do all these things, but very often I fail.

I often feel, like the Red Queen, that:

"HERE, YOU SEE, IT TAKES ALL THE RUNNING YOU CAN DO TO KEEP IN THE SAME PLACE."

I often feel very frustrated with other people, with circumstances, with myself. I feel impotent and de-skilled in so many situations. I fail often and, when I do succeed, I have no measure of that success or of the value of my contribution to it. I often do seem to be running very hard indeed in order to keep in the same place.

I need also to recognise that I will fail, I will be wrong and I cannot measure success. I need to do this in order to be able to fully enjoy the very many lovely, exciting and moving things that happen. Progress may be infinitesimally slow, but it is never really "the same place" and I must allow myself the time and space to appreciate the surroundings.

The White Knight spent a lot of his time in a position I find familiar, of not knowing what day of the week it is or even which way up he is. He is philosophical.

"WHAT DOES IT MATTER WHERE MY BODY HAPPENS TO BE? MY MIND GOES ON WORKING ALL THE SAME".

The problems will always be there.

Much of what I do – most of what I do – I do for myself. In caring for children, I care for the child in me. In caring for a person who is disabled, I look after my own internal disabilities.

I am not so powerful – or so weak – that what I do will have an undue effect – or none at all.

I am one instrument in an orchestra. We may be playing a great symphony or a nursery rhyme, but the sound we produce will depend on us all, the balance of all our efforts.

Working in special education and with people with disabilities leaves me with feelings that echo those of Alice.

"SOMEHOW IT SEEMS TO FILL MY HEAD WITH IDEAS – ONLY I DON'T EXACTLY KNOW WHAT THEY ARE."

I have mentioned some of the difficulties. I would like to finish by sharing some of the joys.

A boy of ten, totally dependent, with no speech, is slowly becoming able to use Blissymbols. This week he said, in symbols "question: God hear no speak?"

I assured him that many people prayed in their heads without speaking and asked if he had something special he wanted to pray for. He answered: "help switch computer, electric wheelchair."

Another Bliss user of fourteen was interested to hear the theory of karma and reincarnation. He said:

"I like die – come-back."

I asked what he would like to come back for.

"I come back no handicap."

What, I asked, would he like to be "next time round?"

"A flower. One, seed under ground. Two, grow up and up. Grow up to sun. Three, beautiful flower."

A ten year old told me how he had seen his father die of a heart attack. He said, "It was a massive heart attack and he had no pain. That was good for him but not for mummy and me. Mummy needed to cry and I held on to her."

I asked if he needed to cry. "Yes," he said "But not all the time. It's alright to feel happy some of the time."

Finally, a fifteen year old told me,

"This school is a community. You've got trust here, adults and kids trust each other."

I will close with the Unicorn's words to Alice:

"IF YOU BELIEVE IN ME, I'LL BELIEVE IN YOU. IS THAT A BARGAIN?"

APPENDIX 5:
Questionnaire for Parents to Help in Planning Teaching Requirements of Children Regarding Cooking Skills

(1) Introduction

This questionnaire is designed to help your child's domestic science teacher in planning what would be most useful for her to learn in becoming self-sufficient in the kitchen.

It is divided into two parts   (a) Your Kitchen
(b) Your Child

(a) Your Kitchen

(i) How high are the work surfaces?
(ii) How high are the taps and what type of handle do they have?
(iii) What is the surface of your cooker? (eg. ceramic hob, rings)
(iv) Do you have a cooker guard?
(v) What type of oven do you have?
(vi) Where are the controls for the oven?
(vii) How high is the oven from the floor?
(viii) Where are the controls for the rings (gas/electric)?
(ix) Where are the controls for the grill?
(x) How high is the fridge door handle and the shelves?
(xi) Do you have a
- food processor/mixer?
- Microwave?
- can opener? (eg. electric)
- Specially adapted handles for cooker controls?
- Specially adapted handles for utensils?
- Plate guards?
- Non-stick saucepans?
- Non-stick cooking surfaces?
- Non-slip materials? (eg. mats)

(xii) Please draw a plan or your kitchen, as if seen from above, giving approximate measurements.

An example follows:

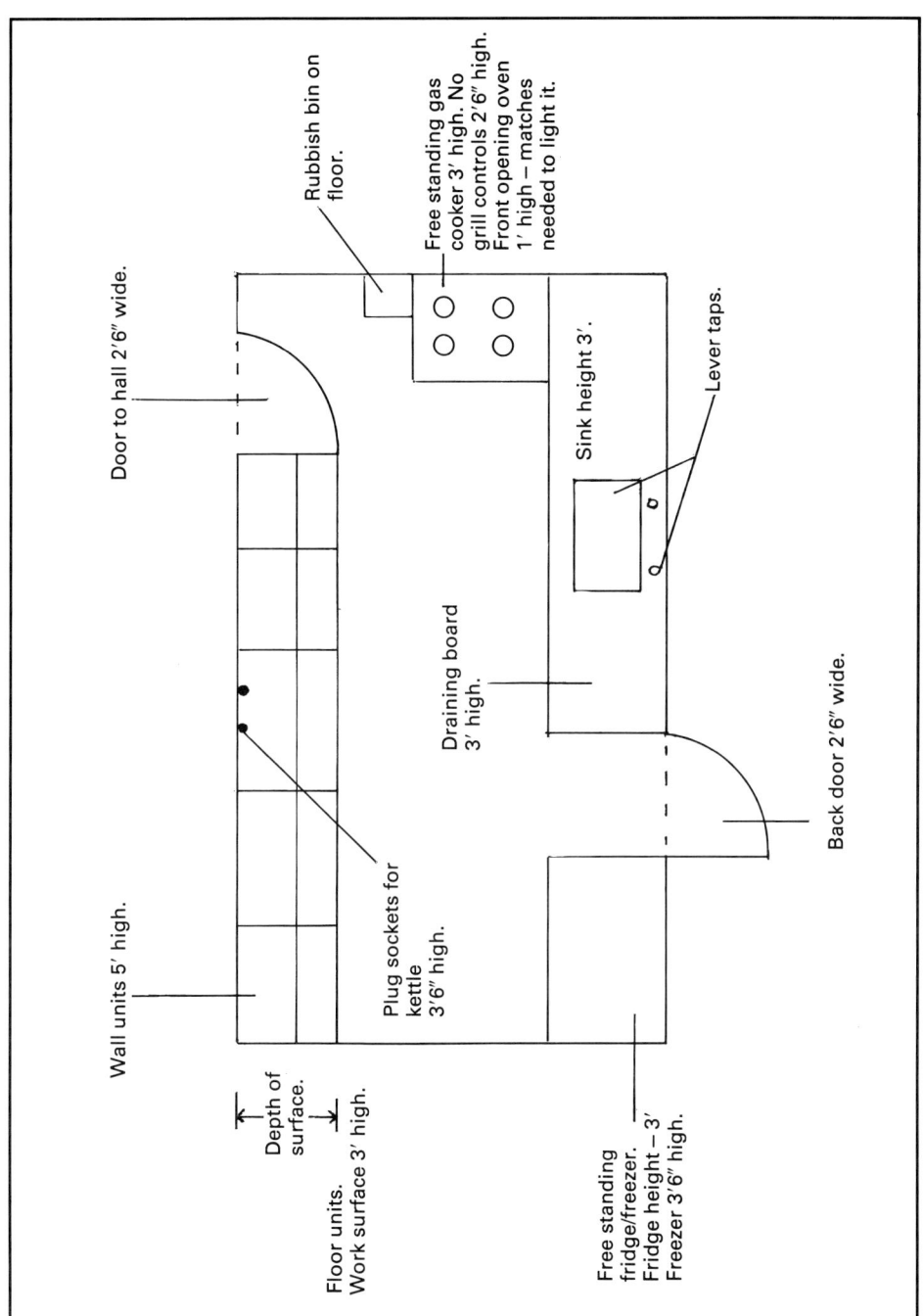

(xiii) Please list:
    (a) any particular skills you would like to teach your child in the kitchen.
    (b) any other specifications in your kitchen that you think may be relevant.
    (c) any special techniques your child uses eg. joint protection methods, precautions because of impaired sensation.
    (d) which special kitchen aids you think your child would find useful? eg.
- jar/bottle openers?
- utensils/cutlery with adapted handles?
- teapot/kettle tippers?
- electric tin openers?
- non-slip mats?
- suction bowls?
- adapted peelers/grators/scissors?
- perching stool?
- tap turners?

(b) Your Child

(i) Can your child reach the sink taps?
(ii) Can your child open a tin?
(iii) Can your child pour accurately?
(iv) Can your child lift a saucepan?
(v) Does your child use mobility aids to move around the kitchen?
(vi) Can your child manage two-handed activities?

Further ideas for adapting kitchens can be obtained from the series "Equipment for the Disabled: Home Management" available from

    Mary Marlborough Lodge
    Nuffield Orthopaedic Centre
    Headington
    Oxford OX3 7LD

    Telephone: (0865) 64811 ext. 272

APPENDIX 6:
Independence Awards for Physically Handicapped Young People

These awards were developed and printed by Diane Bailey in her role as occupational therapist.

(1) Taking Care of Yourself Awards

aim	– to increase progressively the ability to live independently and the awareness of why it is important
qualification for entry	– awards may be gained only by those students with a substantial physical impairment
examination	– requirements at all levels must be strictly adhered to. Tasks must be carried out without any prompting. If the student is not physically capable of doing the task, he/she must show his/her ability to tell exactly how it should be done. Aids can be used if helpful for the task(s)
examiners	– Unit Teacher – School Nurse – Community Occupational Therapist and other individuals when appropriate

Rewards for achievement of the Awards will be:

        Bronze – £3.00 Book Token or "Boots" Token
        Silver – £5.00 Book Token or "Boots" Token
        Gold – £7.00 Book Token or "Boots" Token

(2) Out and About Awards

aim	– to increase progressively the ability to make independent use of community resources and to develop use of leisure time
qualification for entry	– as above
examination	– as above
examiners	– as above

Rewards for achievement of the Awards will be:

        Bronze – £3.00 Book Token
        Silver – £5.00 Book Token
        Gold – £7.00 Book Token

TAKING CARE OF YOURSELF

BRONZE

1. For at least one week, choose what clothes you will wear each day and lay them out the night before.
2. Show you are able to undress and dress yourself.
3. Show you are able to manage your own toilet care as needed.
4. Make a hot drink and wash up after a meal.
5. Make a phone call and know how to contact emergency services.
6. Hang up your clothes, pick up objects from the floor and empty a bin for one week.

Signed

Date Achieved

24.COT.7a
5.7.83

TAKING CARE OF YOURSELF

Date Achieved	Signed	SILVER
		1. Carry a key to your home and use it.
		2. Sew on a button or do a simple mending job.
		3. Make your bed daily for a week.
		4. Show you are able to wash your hair.
		5. Describe the health problems that may be associated with your condition and take necessary precautions.
		6. Plan and prepare a nutritious snack using a kitchen tool or aid and wash up.
		7. Show your ability to use the telephone directory and take a phone message.

24.COT.7b
5.7.83

TAKING CARE OF YOURSELF

Date Achieved	Signed	GOLD
		1. Wash, dry and iron an item of clothing.
		2. Show you can manage your own incontinence appliance without assistance.
		3. Make a list of all the items you would need to take on a week's holiday and explain your physical requirements for a week away from home (a) as if to a travel agent and (b) as if to a new helper.
		4. Plan and prepare a nutritious meal and wash up.

		5. Arrange a visit to one of the following when you need to go:
		
		    hairdresser or barber
		    dentist
		    G.P.
		    chiropodist
		    optician
		    family planning clinic.

		6. Show how to change an electric plug.
		7. Show a theoretical and practical knowledge of first aid and emergency procedures.

TAKING CARE OF YOURSELF (MODIFIED CRITERIA)

Date Achieved	Signed	**BRONZE**
		1. For at least one week, choose what clothes you will wear each day and arrange to have them laid out the night before.
		2. Explain, as if to a new helper, how you prefer to be dressed and undressed.
		3. Learn to use an aid to personal care (eg. long handled comb or toothbrush).
		4. Instruct someone how to make a hot drink.
		5. Make a phone call and know how to contact emergency services.
		(Physical assistance can be given as required)

TAKING CARE OF YOURSELF (MODIFIED CRITERIA)

SILVER

1. Explain, as if to a new helper, how you manage your toilet care.
2. Explain, as if to a new helper, how to push, fold up, and maintain a wheelchair.
3. Plan a nutritious snack and instruct someone to prepare a snack.
4. Sew on a button or do a simple mending job with minimal assistance.
5. Show your ability to use the telephone directory and take a phone message.

(Physical assistance can be given as required)

Signed

Date Achieved

TAKING CARE OF YOURSELF (MODIFIED CRITERIA)

Date Achieved	Signed	GOLD
		1. Plan a nutritious meal and instruct someone to prepare a meal.

		2. Arrange a visit to one of the following when you need to go:
		
		    hairdresser or barber
		    dentist
		    G.P.
		    chiropodist
		    optician
		    family planning clinic.

		3. Make a list of all the items you would need to take on a week's holiday and explain to a stranger your physical requirements for a week away from home
		
		    (a) as if to a travel agent and
		    (b) as if to a new helper.

		4. Show a theoretical knowledge of first aid and emergency procedures.
		5. Carry a key to your home and instruct someone to use it.
		6. Show how to change an electric plug. (Physical assistance can be given as required)

OUT AND ABOUT

BRONZE

1. Go to a shop on your own and buy a newspaper or a magazine.
2. Write a letter, buy a stamp and post the letter yourself.
3. Visit a public library and borrow a book, record or tape.
4. Visit the Sports Centre and be able to tell what you can do there.
5. Ring the Welfare Benefits Centre or Department of Social Security and arrange for a booklet about where to get help to be sent to you.
6. Find out who to contact to get your wheelchair or callipers repaired.
7. Do something to help someone in your family.

Signed

Date Achieved

OUT AND ABOUT

Date Achieved	Signed	SILVER
		1. Complete an interest check list then discuss how you use your leisure time now and how you would like to in the future.
		2. Go on an errand for someone you know that takes you outside school or home.
		3. Go to the Information Centre or the Citizens' Advice Bureau to find out something you want to know.

		4. Find one of the following shops and go in alone to buy something costing about £1.00:
		
		    chemist
		    booksellers/stationers
		    record/music shop.

		5. Use a lift in a shop or public building and ask for help from shop staff or passers-by when you need it.
		6. Show an understanding of the reasons for taking exercise and explain how you get exercise.

OUT AND ABOUT

GOLD

1. Arrange to go out for a meal in a restaurant (ring ahead to check access, arrange transport; order the meal and pay your bill).

2. Arrange to go to a concert or play or the cinema
   or
   Visit a club you haven't been to before and be able to tell what they do.

3. Arrange to travel somewhere by train or plane.

4. Help on a volunteer project.

5. Show an understanding of the added cost of being disabled and benefits that are available.

Signed

Date Achieved

OUT AND ABOUT (MODIFIED CRITERIA)

Date Achieved	Signed	
		BRONZE
		1. Go into a shop and buy a newspaper or a magazine.
		2. Write a letter, buy a stamp and post the letter yourself.
		3. Visit a public library and borrow a book, record or tape.
		4. Visit the Sports Centre and be able to tell what you can do there.
		5. Ring the Welfare Benefits Centre or Department of Social Security and arrange for a booklet about where to get help to be sent to you.
		6. Do something to help someone in your family.
		7. Find out who to contact to get your wheelchair or callipers repaired.
		(Physical assistance can be given as required)

OUT AND ABOUT (MODIFIED CRITERIA)

SILVER

1. Complete an interest check list then discuss how you use your leisure time now and how you would like to in the future.

2. Go on an errand for someone you know that takes you outside school or home.

3. Go to the Information Centre or the Citizens' Advice Bureau to find out something you want to know.

4. Find one of the following shops and go in to buy something costing about £1.00:

    chemist
    booksellers/stationers
    record/music shop.

5. Use a lift in a shop or public building and ask for help from shop staff or passers-by when you need it.

6. Try using a computer and explain some of its uses.

    (Physical assistance can be given as required)

| Date Achieved | Signed | |

OUT AND ABOUT (MODIFIED CRITERIA)

Date Achieved	Signed	GOLD
		1. Arrange to go out for a meal in a restaurant (ring ahead to check access, arrange transport; order the meal and pay your bill).
		2. Arrange to go to a concert or play or the cinema *or* Visit a club you haven't been to before and be able to tell what they do.
		3. Arrange to travel somewhere by train or plane.
		4. Help on a volunteer project.
		5. Show an understanding of the added cost of being disabled and benefits that are available.
		(Physical assistance can be given as required)

APPENDIX 7:
"Skills for Adolescence" Curriculum and Pilot Scheme

The SKILLS FOR ADOLESCENCE (SFA) curriculum, developed in 1986, is a co-operative programme of Lions Club International, Quest International and TACADE (Teaching and Advisory Council on Alcohol and Drug Education).

The curriculum in 7 units aims to foster skills in:

    Responsibility
    Decision-Making
    Communication
    Self-Confidence
    Goal Setting

SKILLS FOR ADOLESCENCE: PILOT SCHEME – One teacher's experience with young people with physical disabilities and learning difficulties.

It was agreed to introduce the SFA programme into the school curriculum as a pilot scheme in September 1987. The group chosen was a mix of 4th and 5th year pupils and numbered 12. Some of this type of work had been covered in the previous year with some of the older pupils in the group so they were already familiar with working in small groups and/or pairs, looking at personal and family matters and sharing with each other at a fairly deep level, as well as contributing to class discussions.

Much of the material offered in the SFA programme would be new to all members of the group so it seemed a natural progression to introduce the programme at this point even though it was actually planned for a slightly younger age group.

The first aim was to allow the two year groups to get together and to establish a mutual feeling of trust. Secondly, there was a need for each session to be carefully adapted (i) to suit the needs of young people with physical disabilities and (ii) to proceed at a slightly slower pace.

It was useful to have a co-worker alongside particularly as he was able to contribute to the group from a male point of view. He also had the advantage of knowing some of the pupils through the local PHAB Club.

It is difficult to stand back from the work which I have covered with the pupils in the last eighteen months and give a detached opinion about the effect that this type of work has had. Would such maturation have taken place in the pupils regardless of the particular approach taken over this period of time? Tangible proof is not possible, but I feel that the students who have taken part have developed more self-confidence, a greater self-awareness and an ability to assert themselves to take more responsibility than they would otherwise have done. There have over the months been instances where pupils have spoken up and made important decisions for themselves. One case in particular springs to mind, where a 3rd year boy decided that he would like to transfer to the local mainstream High School and showed sufficient determination to convince both parents and staff that this would be beneficial to him. I am doubtful if this would have occurred two years ago.

During a session dealing with put-down statements and behaviour, pupils felt sufficiently at ease not only to open up among themselves, but also to talk with members of staff. As a result of this frank exchange, much better communications have been established between them. After one session which had been highlighting the importance of making others feel appreciated, one of the less able members of the group shared with us that she had tried out the exercise with her family producing very positive results. Several shy members of the group volunteered to take part in a Harvest Festival Celebration and one is left pondering whether the self-confidence came as a result of the ideas engendered in the course. What I can say with conviction is that at the end of most sessions there is a satisfying feeling of having reached out and touched an area within some of the young people, and it would have been impossible to do a couple of years ago when teaching in the traditional style of formal lessons.

APPENDIX 8:
Certificate of Pre-Vocational Education

AIMS

(a) assists the transition from school to adulthood by further equipping the young people with the basic skills, experiences, attitudes, knowledge and personal and social competences required for success in adult life including work

(b) provides individually relevant educational experiences which encourage learning and achievement

(c) provides young people with recognition of their attainments through a qualification which embodies national standards

(d) provides opportunities for progression to continuing education, training and/or work.

CONTENTS

The contents will include:

(i) a core area of activities which will foster the development of skills, knowledge and attitudes

    personal and career development

    industrial, social and environmental studies

    communication

    social skills

    numeracy

    science and technology

    information technology

    creative development

    practical skills

    problem-solving

(ii) vocational studies based upon a modular approach (ie. "a set of experiences and outcomes which may be achieved through a variety of appropriate learning methods")

(iii) additional studies taking up a maximum of 25 per cent of the course time. Within this area students have the opportunity to develop personal interests. (This section is not compulsory, if youngsters wish to focus upon (i) and (ii) they have that choice.)

> The Certificate of Pre-Vocational Education
> In Joint Board for Pre-Vocational Education
> Mansell J. (1985)
> BTEC and CGEL

REFERENCES

ALLEN I (1987)
Education in Sex and Personal Relationships
Policy Studies Institute – Research Report No. 665
Blackmore Press, Feb. 1987

AMERICAN SOCIETY OF HUMAN GENETICS IN SEXUALITY AND HANDICAP
Eds.: Dechesne BHH, Pons C and Schellen AMCM
Woodhead-Faulkner (1985)

AMMA (1983)
Profiles and Records of Achievement
Assistant Masters and Mistresses Association, Dec. 1983

ANDERSON F J (1982)
Self-Concept and Coping in Adolescents with a Physical Disability
Issues in Mental Health Nursing, 4, pp. 257–274

ANDERSON J (1989)
Health Education Authority Health Skills Project Training Manual
Counselling and Career Development Unit

ANDERSON E M and **CLARKE** L (1982)
Disability in Adolescence
Methuen (1982a): pp. 342–349; (1982b): p. 49; (1982c): p. 99; (1982d): p. 41

ANDERSON W, **BECKETT** C, **CHITWOOD** S and **HAYDEN** D (1985)
Next Steps: Planning for Employment – A Workshop for Parents
Coalition Quarterly, Vol. 4, No. 4
Available from: Federation for Children with Special Needs, 312 Stuart Street, Boston, MASS 02116

BABUSCIO J (1988)
We Speak for Ourselves
SPCK Publications

BANDURA A (1977)
Social Learning Theory
Englewood Cliffs, NY: Prentice-Hall

BARKER M (1984)
Conductive Education
Therapy Weekly, Feb. 9, 1984: p. 6

BLACKHAM (1978)
Education for Personal Autonomy
Bedford Square Press and British Association for Counselling, 1978

BOOKIS J (1983a)
Beyond the School Gate
RADAR (1983b): p. 14

CHAPKIS W (1986)
Beauty Secrets: Women and the Politics of Appearance
The Women's Press

CHERNON K (1986)
The Hungry Self
Virago

CASPAR C (1987)
The C P Pre-School Child in Conductive Education
Conductive Education Association Journal, No. 2, Autumn 1987

COOPER J A and **BJORLING** B J (1981)
Individualized Education Programs for Multiply Handicapped Students
pp. 21–25
Viewpoints in Teaching and Learning, Vol. No. 57, Winter 1981

DEATRICK J A (1984)
It's Their Decision Now: Perspectives of Chronically Disabled Adolescents Concerning Surgery
Issues in Comprehensive Pediatric Nursing, 7, pp. 17–31

DENZIN P (1970)
The Research Act
Butterworth

DESSENT T (1984)
What is important about Portage
NFER – Nelson

DICKSON A (1982)
A Woman in Your Own Right
Quartet

DORNER S (1976)
Adolescents with Spina Bifida – How they See their Situation
Archives of Disease in Childhood, 51, pp. 439–444

DORNER S (1977)
Sexual Interest and Activity in Adolescents with Spina Bifida
J Child Psychol. Psychiat., Vol. 18, pp. 229–237

GAIR N (1988)
Duke of Edinburgh's Award Handbook
Duke of Edinburgh's Award, June 1988

DUNHAM J (1987)
Caring for the Pastoral Carers
Pastoral Care, Feb. 1987

EDWARDS G (1984)
Helping and Hindering
Changes: J. Psychology and Psychotherapy Association, Vol. 3, pp. 20–23

FAIRCHILD S L (1976)
Achievement, Motivation, Self-concept and Independence Training of Physically Handicapped Children
Dissert. Abstracts Int., 28, 2605–B

FELDMAN W S and **VARNI** J W (1982)
A Parent-Training Programme for the Child with Spina Bifida
Spina Bifida Therapy, Vol. 4, No. 2

FELDMAN W S, **MANELLA** K J and **VARNI** J W (1983)
A Behavioural Parent-Training Programme for Single Mothers of Physically Handicapped Children
Child: care, health and development, 1983, 9, pp. 157–168

FINKELSTEIN V (1981)
To Deny or Not to Deny Disability
In: *Handicap in a Social World*
Eds.: A Brechin, P Liddiar and J Swain, The Open University

FOSTER J E *et al.* (1977)
Guidance, Counselling & Support Services for High School Students with Physical Disabilities
Technical Education Research Center, Cambridge, Mass. USA

FRY E (1986)
Giving Disabled People an Equal Chance
Spastics Society

GOULD M (1986)
Self-Advocacy: Consumer Leadership for the Transition Years
Journal of Rehabilitation, Oct.–Dec.

GOULD M and **McTAGGART** N (1988)
Self-advocacy for Transition: Implications of Student Leadership Potential Today
Self-advocacy Training Project of Maryland

GOW L and **HORBAN** S (1986)
Consideration in Implementing Independent Living Skills Programs in Sheltered Workshops during Financially Difficult Times
Australian Disability Review

GRESHAM F M (1981)
Social Skills Training with Handicapped Children: A Review
Review of Educational Research, 51, pp. 139–176

HAIGHT S L and **FACHTING** D D (1986)
Materials for Teaching Sexuality, Love and Maturity to High School Students with Learning Disabilities
J of Learning Disabilities, Vol. 19, No. 6, June/July

HARRE R and **SECORD** P (1972)
The Exploitation of Social Behaviour
Blackwell

HARVEY D H P and **GREENWAY** A P (1984)
The Self-Concept of Physically Handicapped Children and their Non-handicapped Siblings: An Empirical Investigation
J Child Psychol. Psychiat., Vol. 25, No. 2, pp. 273–284

HENDRY L B (1983)
Growing Up and Growing Out
Aberdeen University Press

HENDRY L and **MARR** D (1985)
Leisure Education and Young People's Leisure
Scottish Educational Review, Vol. 17, p. 2

HERSOV J and **COOPER** D (1986)
We can Change the Future
National Bureau for Handicapped Students

HEUMANN J *et al.* (1987)
Taking Charge of your Life
Center for Independent Living, USA

HOLGATE L (1985)
Young People with Spina Bifida and/or Hydrocephalus
Association for Spina Bifida and Hydrocephalus

HOPSON B and **SCALLY** M (1981)
Lifeskills Teaching, p. 21
McGraw-Hill

HOPSON B and **SCALLY** M (1981a)
Lifeskills Teaching Programmes No. 1
Lifeskills Associates, pp. 50–52

HOPSON B and **SCALLY** M (1982)
Lifeskills Teaching Programmes No. 2
Lifeskills Associates, p. 199

HOPSON B and **SCALLY** M (1987)
Lifeskills Teaching Programmes No. 3
Lifeskills Associates, (1987a): p. 12; (1987b): p. 15; (1987c): p. 159

HURST M (1985)
Could Schools do More for Leavers?
B J of Special Education, 12(4) Dec.

HUTCHINSON D and **TENNYSON** C (1986)
Transition to Adulthood: A Curriculum Framework for Students with Severe Physical Disability
Further Education Unit (FEU)

ILLICH J (1975)
Limits to Medicine: Medical Nemesis
Penguin

ILLICH J *et al.* (1977)
The Disabling Professions
Marion Boyars, London

JONES T, **MINNS** A and **WRIGHT** C (1988)
An Evaluation of the Sheltered Placement Scheme
Department of Employment (March 1988)

KUBLER-ROSS E (1969a)
On Death and Dying
Tavistock Press

KENNETT E A (1986)
A Case for Providing Art Therapy for Children with Physical Handicaps
Unpublished

KESSELL M et al. (1985)
Adventure Etc. – A Health Promotion Program for Chronically Ill and Disabled Youth
J of Adolescent Health Care, 6, pp. 433–438

KETTLE M (1986)
The Employment of Disabled Teachers
RADAR and Association of Disabled Professionals

KINSEY A C, POMEROY W B, MARTIN C E (1948)
Sexual Behaviour in the Human Male
W B Saunders and Company, Philadelphia and London

KINSEY A C, POMEROY W B, MARTIN C E and GEBHARD P H (1953)
Sexual Behaviour in the Human Female
W B Saunders and Company, Philadelphia and London

KIRKHAM M A, SCHILLING R F, NORELIUS K and SCHINKE S P (1986)
Developing Coping Styles and Social Support Networks: An Intervention Outcome Study with Mothers of Handicapped Children
Child: care, health and development, 1986, 12, pp. 313–323

JEFFREE D M and CHESELDINE S (1982)
Pathways to Independence
Hodder and Stoughton Educational

JOWETT S, HEGARTY S and MOSES D (1988)
Joining Forces – A Study of Links between Special and Ordinary Schools
NFER Research Library Series, NFER – Nelson

LAWLEY P (1985)
The Pastoral Care of Teachers
Pastoral Care, November 1985

LEAHY L (1982)
Barrier to Intimacy for People with Physical Disabilities
Social Work Monographs: Social Work Today

LEESON J and OPOLSKI J (1987)
Parents and Professionals: A Working Relationship
Early Child Development and Care, Vol. 27, 1987

LIDDELL G (1982)
Death of a Child
Nursing (Feb. 1982), pp. 1498–1499

LOUGHARY J W and RIPLEY T M (1978)
Career and Life Planning Guide
Follett, Chicago

LOWE P (1988)
Special Needs in Ordinary Schools Responding to Adolescent Needs
A Pastoral Care Approach, Cassell Education Limited

MacBETH A (1984)
The Child Between: A Report on School–Family Relations in the Countries of the European Community
The Commission of the European Community Studies Collection Education Series No. 13

MACREDIE T and BRADSHAW J (1984)
Teaching Social Skills: Evaluation of an "Independence Week"
Child: Care, Health and Development, 10(3), pp. 181–188 (1984)

McKOWN J M (1986)
Disabled Teenagers: Sexual Identification & Sexuality Counselling
Sexuality and Disability, Vol. 7, No. 1/2, Spring/Summer 1986

McTAGGART N and GOULD M (1987)
Choices and Empowerment towards Adulthood: A Self-Advocacy Manual for Students in Transition
Self-Advocacy Training Project of Maryland

MITTLER H and BUCKINGHAM A (1987)
Getting Ready to Leave
B J of Special Education, Vol. 14, No. 1, 1987

MOSES H, BORRELL K and SILER A
Monograph No. 10: Issues in Developing Peer Counselling Programs
Research and Training Center on Independent Living
University of Kansas, July 1982

MUNDY J and ODUM L (1979)
Leisure
New York: John Wiley

NATHWANI A and PERKINS N (1987)
Disability and Ethnic Minority Communities
GLAD, January 1987

ORBACH S (1978)
Fat is a Feminist Issue
Arrow Press

ORBACH S and EICHENBAUM L (1988)
Bittersweet
Arrow Press

PARKER G (1984)
Training for Continence among Children with Severe Disabilities
Social Policy Research Unit, University of York
B. J. of Mental Subnormality, June 1984, pp. 38–41

PEARCE B *et al.* (1982)
Trainee Centred Reviewing (Research and Development) Series No. 2
Manpower Services Commission

PILON B H and SMITH K A (1985)
A Parent Group for the Hispanic Parents of Children with Cerebral Palsy
CHC, Fall 1985, Vol. 14, No. 2

PRING R (1987)
Lifeskills
Times Educational Supplement, 12.6.87

PRINS H (1974)
Motivation in Social Work
Social Work Today, Vol. 5, No. 2, 18.4.74

QUICKE J (1987)
The Disability Curriculum
Pastoral Care, June 1987

RAZEGHI J A *et al.* (1983)
An Advocacy Curriculum for Total Career Development and Independent Living Skills for Handicapped Students
American Coalition of Citizens with Disabilities, Washington, June 1983

ROGERS C (1967)
On Becoming a Person
Constable, London

ROSENTHAL R and JACOBSON L (1968)
Pygmalion in the Classroom
New York: Holt, Rhinehart and Winston

STATHAM J (1987)
Speaking for Ourselves: Self-Advocacy by People Called Mentally Handicapped
In: *Including Pupils with Disabilities: Curricula for All*
Eds.: Booth T and Swann W
Open University Press, 1987

STEWART W F R (1979)
The Sexual Side of Handicap
Woodhead-Faulkner

SZWED C (1986)
Sharing the Caring: A Discussion of Home/School Liaison
Pastoral Care, June 1986

THOMAS A (in press)
Social Skills and Physical Handicap
In: *Conversation, an Interdisciplinary Perspective*
Eds.: Roger D B and Bull P E
Multilingual Matters

THOMAS A, **BAX** M and **SMYTH** D (in press)
The Social Skill Difficulties of Young Adults with Physical Disabilities
Child: Care, Health and Development

THOMAS A, **BAX** M and **SMYTH** D (1987)
Provision of Support Services for the Handicapped Young Adult
Department of Child Health: Charing Cross and Westminster Medical School, July 1987

TREND U and **NICOLL** A (1987)
Disabled Children in a Comprehensive School
Health at School, Vol. 2, No. 4, Jan. 1987

TSE A M and **OPIE** N D (1986)
Menarche in the Severely Disabled Adolescent: School Nurses' Attitudes, Perceptions and Perceived Teaching Responsibilities
J. School Health, Vol. 56, No. 10, Dec. 1986

TURNBULL A and **RUTHERFORD TURNBULL** H (1985)
Developing Independence
J. Adolescent Health Care, 1985, 6: pp.108–119

WALTERS M J (1982)
The Needs of the Dying Patient and Family
Nursing (Feb. 1982) pp. 1496–1499

WARD M J (1983)
No More Checkers . . . Let's Rap
Teaching Exceptional Children, Summer 1983

WARNOCK REPORT (1978)
London HMSO

WATKINS C (1987)
Parental Involvement in the Upper School
Pastoral Care, June 1987

WEINBERG M S and **WILLIAMS** C J (1974)
Male Homosexuals: Their Problems and Adaptations
New York, Oxford University Press

WHELAN E, **SPEAKE** B and **STRICKLAND** T (1979)
The Copewell Curriculum: Development, Content and Use In: *Learning for Independence*
Eds.: Dean A and Hegarty S
London FEU, Oct. 1984

WHITEHOUSE J (1983)
The Mossford Assessment Chart
NFER – Nelson

WHO (1980)
International Classification of Impairments, Disabilities and Handicaps
World Health Organisation (1980)

WITTE R A (1985)
The Psychosocial Impact of a Progressive Physical Handicap and Terminal Illness (Duchenne Muscular Dystrophy) on Adolescents and their Families
B J of Medical Psychology, 1985, 58: pp. 179–187

WOLFF S (1974)
The Dying Child and His Family
Psychiatry Review

WOOSTER A, **LEECH** N and **HALL** E (1986)
Personal and Social Education in the Special School: A Research and Development Project
Pastoral Care, November 1986

WRIGHT B (1960)
Physical Disability – A Phychological Approach
Harper and Row, pp. 179–182

ZOLA I K (1983)
Towards Independent Living: Goals and Dilemmas In: *Independent Living for Physically Disabled People*
Crewe N M, Zola I K *et al.*
Jossey-Bass, pp. 344–356